Desirée Mays

Opera Unveiled

2004

♪

ART FORMS INC.
Santa Fe · Salt Lake City

Art Forms Inc.
Opera Unveiled 2004 © by Art Forms Inc.
Text copyright © Desirée Mays

Cover design and layout by Pieter Hull
Rear cover photograph by Carolyn Wright

First edition

ISBN 0-9707822-3-3

To order copies of *Opera Unveiled 1999 - 2004*
please send a check for $15 (postage included) to:
Art Forms, Inc., 31 Valencia Loop
Santa Fe, New Mexico 87508
Fax: (505) 466 1908
Email: dmays@attglobal.net

Contents

Simon Boccanegra

Giuseppe Verdi

Shimmering sea!
There Genoa towers above the foaming waves.
— Simon Boccanegra

Mystery and menace make up the troubled heart of Giuseppe Verdi's *Simon Boccanegra*. The libretto describes a melodramatic plot of cloaks, daggers, locked-up daughters, lost children, name-changing, curses, mistaken identities, poison – and, of course, death – all set against a background of riots in which the combatants are constantly changing sides. Verdi's masterpiece embraces all the components of grand opera beginning with the historical Simon Boccanegra and the warring factions of 14th-century Genoa, and ending with an all-too-human story of love, loss, and death.

One constant in the opera is Genoa itself with its great harbor, source of its wealth from the time of the Crusades to the present day; Genoa, a magnificent city whose churches and palaces encircle the bustling harbor. The Ducal palace, where the opera takes place, stills stands close to the water's edge. Verdi loved Genoa, which afforded him respite from the stresses of Milan and its opera politics, and he spent many winters there in his later years.

Verdi was a victim of politics of one kind or another for much of his life. Throughout his career he chafed under the censorship of his work and the restrictions of foreign control over the many principalities that comprised Italy in the early 19th century. Verdi longed for the unification of Italy and actively endorsed independence in many of his operas, most notably *Nabucco*, with its famous chorus "Va pensiero" (Go, thought). The first-night Milanese audience immediately understood the chorus to be a cry for independence not for the exiled Jews of *Nabucco*, but for themselves – a call to arms for a united Italy. The unification movement, known as the Risorgimento, at one point used the acronymic "Viva V.E.R.D.I.!" as their rallying cry, the initials standing not for their beloved composer but for the man they hoped to reinstate as king: Vittorio Emanuele, Re d'Italia.

At the premiere of the first version of *Simon Boccanegra*, in 1857, the Risorgimento had not yet achieved its goal; unification came a few years later, in 1861, when Vittorio Emanuele was indeed proclaimed king of a united Italy. Verdi was persuaded to become a politician when Count Cavour, a leading statesman, convinced him that his presence would lend credibility to the first Italian parliament. Verdi reluctantly agreed, and served one term before extricating himself from the world of politics. He had much in common with the historical Simon Boccanegra – though neither chose to become a statesman, both longed for and worked toward a united Italy. The two powerful men, separated by five centuries, were independent spirits on whom the mantle of political power did not rest comfortably.

The Simon Boccanegra of history lived in Genoa in the 14th century. He and his brothers belonged to the powerful merchant class; his brother Egidio was famed as a sea captain, a privateer, who protected the coast of Genoa from marauding pirates. Earlier generations of the Boccanegra family had escorted knights and their entourages to and from the Crusades in their ships, and had become enormously rich in the process. By the 14th century, the Boccanegras were powerful traders who commanded a large fleet of merchant vessels. Egidio commanded the ships while the shrewd, careful Simon ran the business.

Genoa was in chaos in 1339, due to ongoing fighting among the four leading families of the nobility: the Dorias and the Spinolas, who looked to the Holy Roman Emperor for support, and the Grimaldis and the Fieschis, owners of large plots of land and allied to the Pope and to France. (Members of the last two families appear in the opera.) The merchants, artisans, and common people of Genoa sided with one or another of these warring families, fighting for whichever it was most advantageous to be allied with at any given time.

By 1339, however, there was rioting in the streets, and the ruling families decided it was time for law and order to prevail. They decided to have a man of the people elected – a plebeian, who would represent them and defend their interests, though his actual powers would be little more than those of a mediator. The election was held in the main square, but no one could agree on a suitable candidate until a goldsmith climbed up on top of a wall and shouted, "Here in our midst is Simon Boccanegra, a man of exceptional character. Choose him without more ado." The crowd was surprised, but soon Boccanegra's name was being shouted all over the square. He was brought before them and told he was the unanimous choice of the people. He thanked them for "their mark of goodwill" but declined, until someone shouted "Make him our Doge!" – a position of much greater power. The crowd roared its approval – which suggested that this was not a spontaneous event, but had been well-planned in advance – and Boccanegra gracefully acceded to the will of the people and accepted the new position. The patricians were furious at this turn of events, and fighting broke out at once. Boccanegra acted quickly, quelled the disturbances, and next day was confirmed in the Church of San Lorenzo (the present-day cathedral) as the absolute ruler, the first Doge of the Republic of Genoa.

Boccanegra proved to be a wise and capable ruler. He banished the warring noble families from Genoa, and worked for unity and order without discriminating between nobleman and commoner. He built trade with other countries, assembling in the process a powerful merchant fleet; Genoa prospered under his rule. The banished nobility, however, never forgave him and attempted many times to have him assassinated. As time passed, the fickle Genoese fell out with Boccanegra and, in 1344, the patrician families conspired together to take back the city. Wanting to avoid bloodshed, Boccanegra resigned and fled to Pisa. In his absence, the four families returned, and continued to fight and intrigue until, in 1356, the people asked Boccanegra to restore peace to the city. He was again elected Doge, and again he improved Genoa's fortunes. But his enemies, the dispossessed patricians, were implacable. At a banquet in March 1363, Boccanegra was apparently poisoned, and died painfully some days later. He was succeeded by Gabriele Adorno, his deputy.

Boccanegra's story attracted the playwright Antonio Garcia Gutiérrez, who, as the Spanish consul, visited Genoa in 1843. His play, *Simon Boccanegra*, became the source of Verdi's opera. This was the second time Verdi had used one of Gutiérrez's plays, having adapted *El Trovador* into *Il Trovatore* only a few years earlier.

The libretto, written in 1857 by Verdi's longtime collaborator, Maria Francesco Piave, is an amalgam of history and pure fiction. A war did take place between the leading families of Genoa in the 14th century, Simon Boccanegra was indeed the first Doge of Genoa who later died of poison, and Gabriele Adorno did succeed him. The remainder of the libretto is fictional, drawn mainly from Gutiérrez's play.

The opera, in a Prologue and three acts, is set in the 14th century in: a square in Genoa, on one side of which is seen the Church of San Lorenzo, where the historical Simon Boccanegra was invested as Doge and, on the other side, the Fieschi palace; in the gardens of the Grimaldi palace; and in the council chambers and apartments of the Ducal palace. The Prologue is a somewhat surreal, dream-like vision that provides us with the seeds of the tragedy to come. As the brief, somber introductory music ends, two men are discovered conversing in low, conspiratorial tones. Already, this is a novel beginning for an opera of its time when typically leading characters came onstage and announced their intentions to everyone at large; here the men converse as if they don't want to be overheard. They are planning the election of a leader of the people. Paolo, a goldsmith, proposes Simon Boccanegra, "A hero – one who fought the pirates and chased them from our seas forever, restoring honor to our flag's proud heritage." (Gutiérrez changed historical fact when he made Simon, not his brother, the sea captain.) Pietro, a leader of the people, asks what's in it for him if he promotes this hero. "Honor, power, and riches," Paolo replies. The men agree to lobby for Simon Boccanegra with the people, and Pietro leaves.

Simon enters, seeking Paolo, his friend. "Tomorrow, do you wish to be named our leader?" Paolo asks him. Surprised, Simon declines. Paolo persists and, gesturing to the Fieschi palace, reminds Simon of Maria, the beautiful daughter of the noble Jacobo Fiesco. Paolo knows that Simon is in love with Maria, who bore his child out of wedlock and who, since that time, has been imprisoned in her father's palace. Paolo suggests that if Simon became Doge, Fiesco could not refuse the hand of his daughter in marriage. Simon reconsiders.

When the people assemble to choose their new leader, Paolo comes forward and, echoing his historical counterpart, proposes that Simon Boccanegra be elected. The people repeat the name: "Simon Boccanegra? The sea pirate for our leader?" Paolo tells them the story of the weeping woman inside the palace walls – no one has seen her haunted figure pass by the windows for some time. Suddenly, a mysterious light appears in a window of the palace, and the superstitious crowd withdraws from the stage as Jacobo Fiesco appears. Maria has just died, and her father expresses his grief in the exquisite lament "Il lacerato spirito del mesto genitore" (The tortured soul of a sad father). Fiesco's romanza is compact and direct, punctuated by throbbing timpani at the end of each phrase. Against the "Miserere" of the offstage chorus, Fiesco blames himself for his daughter's death. He begs her, now in heaven, to pray for him, singing "Prega per me" (Pray for me) in a descending step sequence that ends on a magnificent low F. Verdi expresses his compassion for Fiesco's suffering in a melody of extraordinary beauty accompanied by tremolando strings.

Simon enters, exuberant in his belief that, once he is proclaimed Doge, Maria can become his wife. He stops on seeing Fiesco, then runs to him, calls him father, and begs forgiveness. But Fiesco is firm, still deeply hating the man who dishonored his daughter: "Heaven's curse will fall on you who dared to take my child." Simon doesn't understand, and asks Fiesco to strike him dead, if that will placate his anger. Fiesco tells Simon there is only one way he can earn forgiveness: by returning to Jacobo his granddaughter, Maria's daughter. "But that is not possible," Simon replies. He explains that he had taken their infant daughter to a place of safekeeping with an old woman. But one day, when he went to visit them, he found the woman dead and the child disappeared. She is lost. Fiesco swears that there can never be peace between them and walks away, pausing in the shadows, watching from the side of the stage. He has not told Simon that Maria is dead.

Simon approaches the gates of the Fieschi palace and knocks. There is no answer, but the gate, oddly, is open. He enters the dark palace, and is seen taking a lamp from the balcony before disappearing inside. Suddenly, his anguished cry is heard as he discovers the body of his beloved Maria. The watching Fiesco smiles grimly: "The time has come for retribution." The grief-stricken Boccanegra runs out from the palace as the voices of the crowd call out "Boccanegra!" Paolo and Pietro enter at the head of the crowd: "They have appointed you Doge!" The celebrating band contrasts with the despairing Simon's lament. "Paolo," he says brokenly, "There . . . a coffin." "A throne!" Paolo answers, as the act ends on a note of high drama: the celebrating crowd, the broken Boccanegra, and Fiesco's final line, "Simon Doge? Hell fire burns in my breast."

Twenty four years pass between the Prologue and the first act. Boccanegra has served as a wise and noble leader, yet the peace in Genoa is uneasy, made up of ever-shifting allegiances. The leaders of the trouble-making nobility have been exiled, including Jacobo Fiesco and the sons of the Grimaldi family. Unknown to Boccanegra, Fiesco, who now calls himself Andrea, has returned to watch over the Grimaldi estates. Andrea/Fiesco has moved into the Villa Grimaldi with the young Amelia Grimaldi, a child surrounded by deep mystery. One of the few important roles a woman could play in medieval times was as keeper of the family estates while the men were away, banished, exiled, or at war. As long as Amelia Grimaldi lived in the palace, the Doge could not seize their estates.

Act I opens in the gardens of the Grimaldi palace, by the seashore. It is early morning, a calm, peaceful time of half-light just before dawn. Amelia walks alone by the seashore, watching the moon shine on the crests of the waves. In her cavatina, she sings of her sadness at being an orphan, of her memory of the last words spoken to her as a very young child by the old woman who took care of her – for Amelia is, of course, the lost daughter of Maria and Boccanegra and the granddaughter of Fiesco, who now, unknowingly, fills the role of father in her life. But Amelia knows nothing of her history. Her thoughts turn to her early-morning tryst with Gabriele Adorno, the young patrician whom she loves.

Gabriele is heard singing offstage, accompanied by a harp in a style similar to the entrance of Manrico in *Il Trovatore*. In their first duet, the young couple sing words of love. Amelia then gently upbraids Gabriele for meeting at night with Andrea and others to conspire against the Doge. He warns her to be silent, and together they gaze at the sea as the orchestra describes the lapping of the water to trills from the woodwinds, as night turns into day.

Pietro arrives and announces that the Doge is on his way to the palace. Amelia unhappily tells Gabriele that the Doge is coming to ask for her hand in marriage for his favorite, Paolo, whom she hates. She begs Gabriele to go quickly to Andrea to arrange their marriage, then she leaves as Andrea/Fiesco enters. Gabriele at once asks him for Amelia's hand, while wondering about the mystery that surrounds her. Andrea explains that Amelia is not a Grimaldi but an orphan who, when the Grimaldis' daughter died in a convent in Pisa many years before, was taken in by the family to replace the dead child. The Grimaldis gave the orphan child their name in order to protect their wealth and lands while they were in exile; this is the mystery that surrounds her. Gabriele vows that he loves her, Grimaldi or no. Andrea blesses the young man in music reminiscent of Beethoven, as double basses and bassoons underscore solemn church-like chords.

Trumpets announce the arrival of the Doge. Left alone with Amelia, Boccanegra hands her a document pardoning her brothers and allowing them to return from exile. But there is a catch – he intends to ask her to marry Paolo. Amelia tells Boccanegra that Paolo is a villain who is only after her wealth, and that she loves another. She decides to tell the Doge her secret: "I am not a Grimaldi." Boccanegra is taken aback. If not a Grimaldi, then who? She describes the old woman who cared for her, and the seaman who occasionally came to see her when she was small. She has a locket with her mother's picture. Boccanegra is incredulous – could it be? He gently asks if the old woman's name was Giovanna. "Yes." He takes a locket from his breast pocket and holds it up. "Is this your mother?" "Yes." "Maria!" he cries out. "I am Maria," the girl replies. "Sei mia figlia!" (You are my daughter!).

The tension builds, measure by measure, as the lonely Boccanegra questions the young woman, and culminates in a glorious orchestral climax at the moment of recognition. Amelia/Maria is no less ecstatic. Father and daughter embrace as she promises to stay by his side. In moments of nearly unbearable pathos, Boccanegra calls Amelia "Figlia!" over and over again as the orchestra layers the opera's major themes one over the other. Listen for the musical progression toward the climax in this scene, which begins with a violin figure that leads to an oboe introduction, "Orfanella il tetto umile" (I was raised as a humble orphan). The rising passion builds gradually until a great orchestral climax of pizzicato strings is reached, with Boccanegra's emotion-laden "Figlia!" followed by fragile harp arpeggios that move slowly downward, then fade into silence.

At this inopportune moment, Paolo reappears. Boccanegra tells him in no uncertain terms to forget about ever marrying Amelia, but does not tell him why. Paolo, infuriated, refuses to take no for an answer and, in a tense allegro, plans with Pietro to have Amelia abducted that night and taken to the house of Lorenzo (a character we never actually meet).

The great Council Chamber scene, which follows, contrasts sharply with the high drama of the recognition scene, in which Boccanegra is revealed as a tender, loving father. Now, presiding over a meeting of plebeian and patrician councilors, Boccanegra is shown to be a strong leader, a statesman who would end bloodshed and unite the country he loves. This scene was not part of the original opera in 1857, but was written by Verdi's librettist, Arrigo Boito, for the revised version of 1881. The Doge opens the meeting by asking his councilors to approve a peace treaty with the King of Tartary, thus opening up the Black Sea ports to trade with Genoa. The councilors agree. Boccanegra then broaches a more sensitive subject, asking for peace with a fellow Italian state, Venice. He holds up a letter (which still exists) from the poet Petrarch, which warns both Venetians and Genoese that they are about to throw themselves into fratricidal conflict, and states that both are the sons of the same mother, Italy. The councilors will have none of it. They rise to their feet, shouting "War with Venice!"

The debate is interrupted by the sounds of an angry mob pursuing Gabriele and Andrea shouting, "Morte, morte!" (Death, death!) The Doge demands an explanation. Gabriele is brought in, bloodied sword in hand. He explains that he has killed Lorenzo for abducting Amelia the night before. The enraged Gabriele was told by the dying Lorenzo that he had been hired to abduct her by a man of power. Assuming that man to be the Doge, Gabriele lunges at him just as Amelia rushes in and stands between the two men. She confirms that she was abducted and taken to the house of Lorenzo, who, on her insistence that he would die for this act, told Amelia the name of the man behind the plot, then let her go. The crowd – councilors, patricians, and plebeians alike – instantly assumes their fellows to be guilty, and a riot is about to break out when the furious Boccanegra rises to his feet and roars "Fratricidi! Plebe! Patrizi!" (Murdering brothers! People! Patricians! Inheritors of a fierce history! Inheritors only of hatred, while the vast kingdom of the seas is open to you! In the land of your fathers you spill each other's blood. I weep for Genoa and cry for peace, for love!) The crowd's anger dissipates before Boccanegra's impassioned plea. Sensing that Paolo is the guilty party in Amelia's abduction, Boccanegra calls him forward and demands that he assist in catching the criminal. Finally, magnificently and majestically, Boccanegra curses the evildoer "Sia maledetto!" (May he be cursed!). The orchestra accuses the treacherous Paolo in an ominous bass clarinet solo as Boccanegra insists that Paolo repeat the curse. The guilty man cries out, terrified, "Sia maledetto," muttering to himself "Orrore!" (Horror!) as the curtain falls.

Act II takes place in the Doge's chambers in the Ducal palace. Paolo and Pietro are once again conspiring, this time against the Doge. Pietro leaves and, in a soliloquy that presages Iago, Paolo, terrified and infuriated by Boccanegra's curse, determines to have revenge by any means, at any cost. He pours a vial of poison into the Doge's drinking goblet. Then, as minister, he calls before him Gabriele and Andrea/Fiesco, who are being held in protective custody by the Doge. Paolo, knowing Andrea's hate of the Doge, asks him to kill Boccanegra while he sleeps. Andrea refuses to perform such a cowardly act and is returned to prison. Paolo has more success with Gabriele when he tells him that the Doge abducted Amelia for his "own lustful pleasure." The gullible, impetuous Gabriele believes him and swears he will kill Boccanegra. Paolo leaves, and Gabriele agonizes over Amelia's being the Doge's mistress. Amelia enters and Gabriele accuses her of being unfaithful. She admits that she loves the Doge with a pure love, but will not tell Gabriele why.

When the Doge approaches, Amelia hides Gabriele beyond earshot, on the balcony. Father and daughter embrace, and she tells him of her love for Gabriele, entreating her father to pardon him. Boccanegra is distressed – he knows that Gabriele is a patrician in league with his enemies. Amelia leaves as the Doge rests, exhausted. He pours and drinks from the goblet on the table and soon sleeps, thinking of Amelia. Gabriele reappears and would stab the sleeping Boccanegra, but Amelia, suspecting an attack, runs in to protect her father. In the ensuing fast-paced dialogue, Boccanegra tells Gabriele the truth. "You have stolen my treasure and beauty. She is my daughter!" The thunderstruck Gabriele realizes the enormity of his mistake and swears from henceforth to be loyal to the Doge. Cries from outside call for "War and massacre!" Boccanegra sends Gabriele out to quell the riot and to make peace with the people, promising him Amelia should he be successful.

Act III is set in rooms in the Ducal palace, from which the harbor and the sea can be seen. The uprising has been put down, and the Doge is victorious once more. Paolo, on his way to execution, meets Andrea and tells the older man that he has poisoned the Doge. An unaccompanied wedding chorus celebrating the marriage of Amelia and Gabriele is heard offstage. As he is led away to execution, Paolo rails against a fate that gave the woman he wanted to another.

For the proud Andrea/Fiesco, the moment of vengeance has come. The Doge enters, already weakened by the poison. Fiesco confronts him, threatening death. Recognizing his voice, Boccanegra attempts to embrace the man who for so long was his enemy. He tells the startled Fiesco that Amelia, the child Fiesco had watched over for so many years, is actually the daughter of Maria, Boccanegra's daughter, and Fiesco's own granddaughter. Fiesco weeps and sings, in music reminiscent of the opening of Beethoven's

"Moonlight" sonata, of how he hears the voice of heaven in Boccanegra's words. Reconciliation is sweet, heartfelt, overwhelming – and bitter, as Fiesco informs Boccanegra that he has been poisoned. Amelia and Gabriele appear with their wedding guests, their joy complete when Boccanegra tells Maria that Fiesco is her grandfather. Then, as the poison takes hold, the dying Boccanegra calls his children to him, blesses them, names Gabriele as his successor, and empowers Fiesco to see that his wishes are carried out. Boccanegra dies in Amelia's arms as Fiesco addresses the crowd: "People of Genoa! Hail Gabriele Adorno as your Doge." "No, Boccanegra!" they reply. "Boccanegra is dead. Pray for his soul." The opera ends on a somber note as the crowd kneels to pray to the slow tolling of a church bell.

This is the story of Verdi's Simon Boccanegra, a complex character who, in alternating moods of nobility, resignation, nostalgia, loneliness, and tenderness, has much in common with the character of the composer himself.

The path to success for this opera, however, was a particularly thorny one for Verdi since there were two quite different versions, the first from 1857, the second from 1881.

In 1855, on completing *Les Vêpres siciliennes* for Paris, Verdi thought once more about composing an opera based on *King Lear*, a dream he pursued for many years that never came to fruition. After Paris, he returned to his beloved farms and home at Sant' Agata and worked on adapting *Stiffelio* into *Aroldo*, a necessary task to appease the censors. Then, in March 1856, he agreed to compose a new opera for La Fenice in Venice. The subject, *Simon Boccanegra*, was to be taken from Gutiérrez's play and written by Verdi's librettist, Francesco Piave. Traveling constantly, supervising and conducting performances of his operas, Verdi and Piave had little time to collaborate on the new opera, so Verdi asked a friend, Montanelli, to rework some of Piave's scenes. The premiere in Venice in 1857 was not a success. The opera played in a few Italian cities and then was neglected, overshadowed by the success of Verdi's next operas, *Un Ballo in maschera* and *La Forza del destino*.

It was 23 years later when Ricordi, Verdi's publisher, suggested that he take another look at *Simon Boccanegra*. Verdi, now 67 and already thinking of *Otello*, the opera he was to create with Arrigo Boito, was enthusiastic. In what was to be the greatest artistic collaboration of his career, Verdi was eager to work with Boito, a composer, librettist, and theatre critic, who belonged to a new, younger generation of musicians and writers. It seemed appropriate that their partnership should start out with the reworking of *Simon Boccanegra*, an opera that had always been dear to Verdi's heart.

Musically, Verdi was in a very different place when he came to revise this opera in 1880. Moving away from the traditional series of self-contained numbers, he was experimenting with more continuous and dramatically realistic compositional methods. Entrance arias, set pieces, and cabalettas were now outdated, so, for instance, Amelia's Act I cavatina was changed to a cantabile piece, the scoring making the aria a unified whole instead of several different sections, which had been the technique of the early part of the century. Fiesco and Boccanegra's duet in the Prologue demonstrates well Verdi's later style and his masterful grasp of both musical and dramatic needs; the two men's dialogue, thoughts, and feelings are composed in a blend of musical recitative, arioso, parlante, and melody.

There was much to revise. Verdi wrote to Ricordi, "The score as it stands is too sad, too desolate." Boito compared the drama to a rickety table of which only one leg, the Prologue, was sound. Verdi responded, "I admit the table is shaky, but if we adjust the legs a little I think it will stand up." Toward the end of the revisions, Boito wrote, "To go back to the comparison of the table; now it's the fourth leg [Act III] that's unsteady. We must prop it up and use a good deal of cunning so that once it's been put to rights the others don't start to rock again." Verdi agreed "[to] adjust the fourth leg. And to try to straighten out here and there the many crooked legs of my notes."

Boito and Verdi's collaboration progressed rapidly through the winter of 1880. They decided to add an entirely new scene to Act II: the famous Council Chamber scene, in which Boccanegra's greatness, humanity, and statesmanship would be shown. The impetus for this scene came when Verdi remembered "two superb letters of Petrarch's, one written to the Doge Boccanegra and the other to the Doge of Venice reminding them that both were the sons of the same mother, Italy." The second letter stated, "It is fine to defeat an enemy by the test of steel; yet finest of all is to conquer him by greatness of heart and soul." Verdi took these lines to heart; they became the inspiration for the Council Chamber scene and were written into the libretto by Boito.

Many of the 1857 duets were reworked. Of Fiesco and Gabriele's duet in Act I, when Gabriele asks for Amelia's hand in marriage, Verdi said, "The tone should be that of a father blessing his adopted children, a moment that is calm, solemn, religious." For all of Fiesco's anger and bitterness, Verdi bathes this tormented character in compassion when he describes a father's grief at Maria's death in "Il lacerato spirito," and, at the end, in Fiesco's tears at the moment of reconciliation with Boccanegra.

When it came to choosing singers, Verdi had clear ideas about his requirements for the roles. He wrote of Simon, "Calm, poise and a quality of authority on stage are essential for the part of Simon." He found these qualities in Victor Maurel, who sang Boccanegra in 1881, Iago in 1887, and Falstaff in 1893, in three premieres of Verdi's late operas. For the bass role of Fiesco, Verdi required a "voice of steel, deep, audible in the bass register right down to F with something in it that is inexorable, prophetic, sepulchral." His Fiesco in the 1881 version was Eduoard de Reszke. Another baritone role, Paolo, a prototype for Verdi's Iago, was to be defined not by greed but by his hatred and jealousy of Boccanegra. Gabriele was sung by the tenor Francesco Tamagno, who was to sing the first Otello six years later. So already, in *Simon Boccanegra*, the extraordinary partnership of Verdi and Boito, along with the great singers Maurel and Tamagno, was moving toward Verdi's final operas, *Otello* and *Falstaff*. The revised *Simon Boccanegra* premiered at La Scala, Milan in March 1881, this time with resounding success.

Today, the success of any production of *Simon Boccanegra* depends in great part on the dramatic and vocal abilities of the singers who portray Boccanegra and Fiesco. Boccanegra is one of the most dramatically demanding and vocally challenging baritone roles in the entire Verdian repertoire. One of the finest recordings of the opera includes Tito Gobbi and Boris Christoff in those roles, with Gabriele Santini conducting. Gobbi said of *Boccanegra*, "I cannot describe the joy, the respect, the sheer love with which I have tried to serve this great work."

Beyond the musical greatness of *Simon Boccanegra*, other, much more personal issues lie at the heart of this opera about fathers. Verdi wrote many times on the subject of the love of a parent for a child, typically one lost or suffering: of Rigoletto and his dishonored and ultimately murdered daughter, Gilda; of the tortured relationship of a mother and son in *Il Trovatore*; in Aida's love of Amonasro; even of Violetta, in *La Traviata*, who longs to be a daughter to Germont, father of her lover. For Verdi, the most terrible time of his life occurred when, in his 20s, his young wife Margherita and their two very small children all died within a few months of each other, leaving him desolate. He never got over their loss; 17 years later, when he composed music about a father's loss of his daughter in *Simon Boccanegra*, the music came from the depths of his own longing. In these operas, Verdi explored over and over again the theme of loss; it was never far from his mind or his creativity, never forgotten, never resolved. Perhaps much of the attraction of *King Lear*, an opera he always wanted to compose, was the theme of Lear's love for Cordelia, his daughter.

Another aspect of Verdi's life is addressed in *Simon Boccanegra* in the relationship between Boccanegra and Fiesco, two mighty men who become enemies over the loss of a daughter and who, years later, are reconciled through the love of that same daughter. When Verdi was a young man, his mentor and surrogate father was Antonio Barezzi. It was Barezzi's daughter, Margherita, whom Verdi married and lost. Years after Margherita's death, Verdi brought his new love, Giuseppina Strepponi, to his home in the small town of Busseto, where his father-in-law lived. Barezzi and the townspeople would have nothing to do with Verdi or Strepponi at first, but over the years, Barezzi came to accept Strepponi, even love her as a daughter, and the two men were reconciled. This reconciliation is echoed in the final duet between Boccanegra and Fiesco.

Verdi and Strepponi spent most of their winters together by the sea in Genoa. The images and sounds of the sea, ever-present in *Simon Boccanegra*, are the opera's unifying force. Act I describes the sea at dawn, all shimmering strings and gentle movement. The orchestral accompaniment to Amelia's cavatina paints the waves dancing happily, rising and falling gently as the orchestral colors shift and lighten. When the young lovers gaze at the "foaming waves," Gabriele speaks to Amelia in images of the sea: "Do not try to fathom the mysteries of hate, but rest in the harbor of my love." At the end, the sea is again the focus, when the dying Boccanegra sings, over softly undulating strings, "To breathe the fresh wind of heaven blowing from the harbor. The salt wind, how it brings back memories!"

The sea surrounds this opera, alternately revealing and washing over the stories of the men and women who walked its shores over the centuries: the generations of seafaring Boccanegras, who traded and fought on the Mediterranean; the historical Simon Boccanegra, first Doge of Genoa; the fictional Boccanegra, surrounded by the scheming Grimaldis and Fieschis, whose palaces grace the harbor's edge; and Amelia and Gabriele, who sing of their love as they watch the waning moon over the sea. On walks by the side of the great harbor, Verdi, accompanied by Strepponi, perhaps conceived of and heard in his head the great sea-storm that would open *Otello*. The Ducal palace, the cathedral of San Lorenzo, the harbor – all exist today, quiet observers of the inevitable tides that flow in and out over time and history.

Petrarch said it well all those years ago when he wrote, on seeing the harbor of Genoa, "And the boatman, lost in admiration of the new sights before him, let the oars fall from his hands and, marveling, stayed the boat in mid-course."

Characters

Simon Boccanegra, a sea captain of the Genoese republic	Baritone
Jacopo Fiesco (Andrea), a Genoese noble	Bass
Paolo Albiani, a Genoese goldsmith	Baritone
Pietro, a popular leader	Baritone
Gabriele Adorno, a Genoese gentleman	Tenor
Maria Boccanegra (Amelia Grimaldi)	Soprano

Bibliography
Budden, Julian, *The Operas of Verdi*, Vol. 2, Clarendon Press, Oxford, 1992.
John, Nicolas, ed., *Simon Boccanegra*, English National Opera Guide 32, Riverrun Press, New York, 1985.
Morgan, Christopher, *Don Carlos and Company*, Oxford University Press, 1996.
Osborne, Charles, *The Complete Operas of Verdi*, Da Capo Press, New York, 1969.

Don Giovanni

Wolfgang Amadeus Mozart

When one skips a stone over the surface of the water, it skips lightly for a time, but as soon as it ceases to skip, it instantly sinks into the depths; so Don Juan dances over the abyss, jubilant in his brief respite. – Kierkegaard

Is the character of Don Giovanni the essence of the life-force or a serial rapist? A mere philanderer, a libertine, a rake whiling away the final days of a dying age – or a tortured soul seeking the unattainable? Evil incarnate, or the personification of exuberant sex?

Simultaneously everyman and no man, Don Giovanni is an ineffable force made irresistible by the creative genius of Wolfgang Amadeus Mozart. Captured as long as the music lasts in Mozart and Lorenzo da Ponte's *dramma giacosa*, he is the central force that holds together those other characters whose lives have little meaning without him: Donna Anna, his ideal; Elvira, his complementary opposite; and Leporello, his shadow. He loves and deceives them all.

Tomes have been written about Don Giovanni/Don Juan in an effort to grasp the myth's significance and meaning, but one might as well try to catch hold of a wisp of a cloud. Don Giovanni exists only in the moment of performance – in Mozart, who breathes life into his reprobate hero each time a conductor lifts his baton and opens the opera with the chilling chords that signify the Don's nemesis, the stone statue. The essential character of Don Juan has changed little over time, but the myth has evolved since its first appearance in the 16th century.

Don Juan was first portrayed by a Spanish monk, Tirso de Molina (1584–1648), in his play *El Burlador de Seville, y convidado de piedra* (The Trickster of Seville and the Guest of Stone), which tells the story of the seductions of Don Juan Tenorio and his subsequent descent into hell. All of the major ingredients of the tale are found in Molina's plot: the reckless seducer who attacks a noblewoman, his valet who aids and abets him, the father murdered by the seducer while attempting to protect his daughter, the hero who invites the stone statue of the father to dinner, and the statue itself, which drags Don Juan off to hell. In Molina's version there is no talk of love – the Don's motivating force is simply to seduce, with no pity for the women he dishonored. Molina's story is in two distinct parts: a catalogue of Don Juan's seductions, and the story of the stone statue. The supernatural element was always a component of the early plays, as was music; Molina included a number of songs for the dancing villagers, a serenade for Don Juan, and table music for the last scene.

Hell, in the 16th century, was deemed an appropriate place for Don Juan, a blasphemer, heartless philanderer, and murderer. The archetypal Don scorned God and the devil, monarchs and men. (Women didn't make it onto that list!)

The story of Don Juan was written to demonstrate that sins must be punished. The vengeful triumph of death over the trickster who ridiculed God and religion was the ultimate retribution demanded by the God he defied. When Molina's play reached Italy, commedia dell'arte troupes used the story as a highly successful comedic plot for their improvisational street shows. In France, Molière wrote his play *Don Juan ou le festin de pierre* (Don Juan or The Stone Statue) in 1665, focusing on the libertine and atheistic aspects of Don Juan's character. In this version, the Don is a dissolute French nobleman; Molière also brings the other characters to life by exploring the emotional reactions of Don Juan's victims. By 1713, fairground versions of the story, also called *comédie en chansons*, appeared in Paris with improvised mime and popular songs. One such version proposed that, in hell, Don Juan was to be a puppet forced to play out his seductions eternally.

Perhaps the greatest Romantic interpretation of the myth was written in 1813, by E.T.A. Hoffman, in *The Tales of Hoffman*. A traveler – Hoffman himself – arrives in a provincial German city and retires early to his room, where he hears the sounds of an orchestra tuning up. He is told that the town's theatre is next door, and that a hidden door will take him directly to Box 23. Hoffman hurries to the box, arriving at the start of the overture to Mozart's *Don Giovanni*. He is surprised when the music, played with impeccable mastery, conjures up visions of "red-hot claws of fiery demons looming menacingly over the lives of happy mortals." The curtain rises, and Don Giovanni storms onstage with Donna Anna in hot pursuit. "Her eyes flash love and scorn, hatred and despair. Her dark hair streams over her neck. Her heart throbs, she is grievously betrayed." The handsome, sinister Don seems reluctant to tear himself away: "Is it the inner conflict of love and hate that robs him of his strength and courage? The magic of the serpent

[Satan] is his, and never a woman upon whom he has cast his gaze, but is driven, by a mysterious spell, to make for her own destruction." Donna Anna's father, hearing his daughter's cries, runs to her aid and, in the fight that follows, dies on Don Giovanni's sword.

As Hoffman continues to watch the first act, he becomes aware that someone has joined him in the box, though does not turn to see who his companion is. He feels "a soft warm breath across the back of my neck and hears the rustle of a silk dress." When the curtain falls he turns and, to his amazement, finds "Donna Anna standing behind me, clad in the very costume I had just seen onstage. She fastened her piercing, soulful gaze on me." As they speak, the traveler wonders vaguely how she could be on the stage and in his box at the same time. As they talk, he is at first speechless, then ecstatic. Music is her entire life, she explains. When she sings, she understands many things that words cannot express. But she knows that the traveler, a composer himself, understands her. She knows his music, "For I have sung you; I am your melodies." The theatre bell rings. "A slight pallor drained the color from her face, she clasped her hand to her heart and whispered, 'O unhappy Anna, now your most fearsome times are at hand.' " She vanishes. As Hoffman immerses himself once more in the opera and Donna Anna's aria, "Non me dir" (Say no more), he feels "a glowing kiss burn my lips, a kiss like a long note sustained by an endlessly thirsty longing."

The opera ends, and Hoffman returns to his room in a state of nervous excitement. At midnight, unable to sleep, he takes a small writing desk from his room into Box 23 to write a letter to a friend about the evening's events. He describes Don Giovanni: "Fitted out by Nature and given a close kinship with the divine ... a powerful splendid body; an education that kindles perceptions of the supreme, a profound sensibility, a quick intelligence. Believing he would find transcendence through love, he learned early that reality could never match his ideal so he found all earthly life dim and flat. Every enjoyment of woman was no longer the satisfaction of his sensuality but a rather contemptuous mockery of nature and the creator." Could Anna redeem him? "They met too late when he was only filled with a devilish desire to corrupt her." And corrupt her he did, for "when he fled, the deed was done." For Anna "the flames of a superhuman sensuality consumed her innermost being like a fire from hell making resistance impossible." Once more, Hoffman hears Anna's "Non me dir" echoing in the darkened theatre; it is 2 AM. Anna's soft fragrance seems to surround him.

Next morning, sitting in the inn, Hoffman overhears a conversation about Donna Anna and asks about her. "I hope she isn't seriously ill? We shall hear her again soon?" An old man replies, "That's not likely. You see, the Signora died at exactly two o'clock this morning."

This version of the myth is high romanticism – the dream-like, impossible interactions, the phantasmagorical Box 23, the supernatural appearance of Donna Anna, the final shocking revelation. Hoffman tells us that Donna Anna, like the Don himself, has the highest aspirations and a "thirst for the unattainable." When Don Giovanni dies, she, too, must die, for there is nothing left to live for. She will follow him to hell.

When it was published, Hoffman's tale provoked a furor of discussion amongst the musical cognoscenti on the issue of Anna's seduction. Mozart and da Ponte do not reveal what happens offstage in Anna's bedroom, during the overture. As she enters, running and holding on to the Don, the first lines da Ponte gives her are ambiguous: "No, you shan't escape! I will never let you go!" Because she hates or loves him? "Be quiet," the Don replies, "you shall not know who I am!" Wagner and Berlioz believed she had succumbed; the common consensus of the 19th century, however, was that she had not. This is one of the opera's more tantalizing, unresolved questions, and different answers shed different lights on Donna Anna's motivations in later scenes. But more of Donna Anna later.

Many versions of the myth in the Romantic era presented variations on the theme of Don Juan, among them Mérimée's *Les Ames de Purgatoire* in 1834, Alexandre Dumas *père*'s *Don Juan de Marana* in 1836, and José Zorilla y Moral's *Don Juan Tenorio* in 1844. Zorilla's story is interesting in that it is one of the very few versions in which, at the end, Don Juan is redeemed. It is also the version that most closely evokes the flavor of Spain; the play has remained enormously successful, and can still be seen in Spanish theatres each November, on All Souls' Day.

Zorilla's play is set in the 1550s, a little later than Molina's original, and opens with four masked men: Don Juan, his friend Don Luis, and their fathers, who sit a little way off, listening. The young men have come together to compare notes. A year earlier, they made a pact to see "which could commit more evil in a year," and Don Juan is clearly the winner. They invent new categories for the conquest of women; Don Juan must seduce a novice in a convent, and the intended bride of a friend. He replies that that will take all of six days to accomplish: "One to make love to them, another to enjoy them, another to get rid of them, two to replace them, and an hour to forget them." He informs his friend that the ravished bride-to-be will be Don Luis's own betrothed, Doña Ana.

True to his word, Don Juan seduces first the novice, then Doña Ana, only to discover that, overcome by her innocence, he has fallen in love with her. When her father, the Comendador, confronts the seducer, Don Juan shoots him, abandons Ana, and escapes. Years later, he returns to Seville to visit the family cemetery and finds, to his surprise, a statue of Doña Ana, who died of a broken heart. Don Juan confesses to the statue that he had truly loved her. He leans against the tomb with tears in his eyes; when he looks up, the statue has gone, and in its place he sees Doña Ana's spirit. She tells him that, because she still loves him, God has decreed that she must stay by the tomb until his return. Unafraid, Don Juan dismisses her spirit, then turns to invite the stone statue of her father to dine with him. The statue offers Don Juan his hand (as happens in all versions of the myth) and begins to pull Don Juan to hell. "Have mercy!" the Don cries. "It is too late," the statue replies. At this moment the spirit of Doña Ana takes his free hand and (from the stage directions): "Flowers and perfume surround them. Doña Ana falls on a bed of flowers, Don Juan falls at her feet and both die. From their mouths their souls issue forth in the form of two bright flames which disappear in space as music plays and the curtain falls."

The gothic ending suggests that Don Juan is redeemed by the love of a woman, a theme that would be taken up again and again by writers and composers of the Romantic era. In this perfectly Catholic morality play, the Don's soul, regardless of his sinful life, is saved because, at the last moment, he truly repents. The Spanish came to love this version of the myth. For men, the attractive, passionate, devoted lover (for all of the two days allotted) was brave and courageous, a macho man to imitate. Often presented in Spanish productions swirling a great cape with the panache of a matador, this Don became a larger-than-life hero who, in his search for the perfect woman, was more to be emulated than criticized. He was a hero, a man who would die to defend his honor and lived only for his own pleasure, who was not intimidated by either God or stone statues. Nor did he have to pay the price of an eternity in hell because, at the last moment, he threw himself on God's mercy and thus found salvation. For women, Don Juan came to represent the husband or lover redeemed by sacrifice and love. Some things do not change; Don Juan can still be found in the streets of Seville, calling out to pretty women.

Mozart and da Ponte produced their *Don Giovanni* in 1787. Living at the end of the 18th century, they bridged the Classical and Romantic periods of literature, poetry, and music, as well as the worlds of the *ancien régime* and the Enlightenment. Don Juan was a popular theme – there were no fewer than three other productions based on the same story playing at that time in Vienna – and da Ponte was busy writing libretti for Martin y Soler and Salieri. When asked by the Emperor Joseph how he managed to do it all, da Ponte replied, "I shall write for Martin in the morning, Salieri in the afternoon, and Mozart in the evening." He took as his model a current version of the opera, Gazzaniga's *Il Convitato di piedra* (The Stone Guest), with a libretto by Bertati, whose words he heavily "borrowed" for his own libretto. In the 18th century, such plagiarism was quite acceptable.

Mozart took up the task lightly and composed the opera quickly; it is said that he wrote the great overture only the night before the premiere. Mozart calls his opera a *dramma giacosa* – a mix of *opera seria* and *opera buffa* in which Donna Anna, Donna Elvira, Don Ottavio, and the Commendatore clearly fall into the *seria* category, while Leporello, Zerlina, and Masetto belong to the *buffa* tradition. The baritone Don himself straddles both worlds – he is a *mezzo carattere*, or middle character.

The setting of da Ponte's libretto is intriguing. The characters meet in no set time or place but somewhere out of doors, on streets, in gardens, or cemeteries; only the final banquet scene is indoors, in a somewhat neglected, surreal mansion. In production, these effects can be achieved with a stage set of a movable street bordered by doors that open and close, going nowhere. The great lover is found dining alone at the end with only his gluttonous servant for company, while a little onstage quartet plays, of all things, themes from *The Marriage of Figaro*. The characters meet and pass in a disheveled landscape in which locations that should be distant from one another are suddenly seen side by side – a cinematic technique long before its time.

Director Jonathan Miller describes the opera's characters as "demented banshees weightlessly haunting an abandoned city." They seek to be somewhere else until the opera gradually converges on itself, spinning wildly until the death of Don Giovanni, at which point the action abruptly stops. The spell is broken, the excitement is over. It is time to go home. Without the Don to hold them together, the other characters cease to exist. We are no longer interested in them. Donna Anna tells Ottavio she will marry him – in a year's time. Donna Elvira will "enter a convent, there to end my life!" Zerlina and Masetto go home to dinner together, and Leporello plans to go to the inn to find himself a better master.

Who are these other characters? We have already met Donna Anna. In her aria "Or sai chi l'onore" (Now you know who sought to steal my honor), she describes her midnight visitor to her fiancé, Don Ottavio: "I was alone when I saw a man, wrapped in his mantle, enter my room. I took him to be you. He drew near and attempted to embrace me. I tried to free myself, I screamed." The stranger tells her, "Who I am you shall not know." The man without a name escapes her, kills her father, then disappears into thin air once the murder is done. Donna Anna instructs her fiancé to find and kill her assailant, her father's murderer, for she will have vengeance. Then she tells him they must wait a year before they can be married, for now she is in mourning. She needs time to consider. We, too, need time to consider. Is Donna Anna the chaste, pure, honorable young woman she appears to be? Or has she fallen for the man who came unbidden to her bed?

No sooner has Donna Anna vented her fury (for whatever

reason) than another distraught woman appears on the scene. This time it is Donna Elvira, whom Don Giovanni actually married, come to pursue her absent husband. "Who can tell me where that wretch is? Let him beware who left me, his vows of love denied" (Ah! Chi me dice mai). Donna Elvira has traveled alone overnight on a coach and arrives exhausted, crumpled, and vengeful. Suitcase in hand, she is set down unceremoniously on a street. Don Giovanni greets her approach in the early morning half-light with the words "I scent a woman," then takes cover to see who she is. He decides to comfort what he takes to be an attractive woman who has been deserted by her lover, steps from the shadows, and the two instantly recognize one another. The surprised Don tells Elvira that his servant, Leporello, will explain everything, then disappears. The bewildered Elvira is then subjected to the Catalogue aria, in which Leporello reads her the list of Don Giovanni's 2,065 conquests. She is devastated. Soon, she too is crying "Vengeance!"

Alone and abandoned, Elvira is near madness with the pain of her shame and dishonor. Hate, revenge, despair, and love are all bound up in her heart, and all are expressed violently during the course of the opera. Elvira stalks Don Giovanni – she is the only one who will not let him escape. His counterpart in cunning, she foils his escapades from the moment of her arrival, but ultimately it is she who finds compassion in her heart and begs him to repent before it is too late.

The Danish philosopher Søren Kierkegaard was fascinated by Elvira, and imagined her seduction in his book *Either/Or*. He writes, "I took a walk in one of the romantic valleys of Spain, my eye fell on a cloister high up on the peak of a mountain. My guide told me it was a convent known for its strict discipline." Hearing a noise on the path above him, he saw that "It was a knight who hurried past. How handsome he was, how light his step, yet so full of energy; and yet so evidently in flight; he turned his head to look back. It was Don Juan. He was soon lost to sight; my eye was fixed upon the cloister when I saw high up on the mountain a feminine figure. In great haste she ran down the path, but the way was steep and it seemed she would tumble down the mountain. She came nearer. Her face was pale, only her eyes blazed terribly, her body was faint, her bosom rose and fell painfully, her disheveled locks streamed loose in the wind, her nun's veil was torn and floated out behind her, her thin white gown would have betrayed much to a profane glance had not the passion in her countenance turned the attention of even the most depraved of men upon itself."

This was Elvira, a noblewoman abducted from the mountain convent for three days before Don Juan/Don Giovanni abandoned her. She has lost everything, has now no refuge except with him, and pursues him because she loves him. Fierce one moment, fainting the next, she oscillates between these extremes, seeking him endlessly, eternally, one of Jonathan Miller's "demented banshees" haunting the vacant space that is Don Giovanni. Her obsession and rapid shifts of mood, perfectly reflected in Mozart's music, suggest that she has been brought to the edge of insanity.

Confronting the Don at every turn, Elvira fights for her love. For him she has thrown away eternal happiness, and now she demands revenge. She is a worthy opponent. Even Don Giovanni must have seen Elvira's transformation, from one of many unremembered convent girls he seduced, into a woman armed with passion, hate, and love – a force not easily dismissed. Condemned to a life of restless wandering, Elvira continues to hope; when her hope dies, as it does with the Don's death, she says, "I will return to the convent, there to end my life."

There is a third victim in this day in the life of Don Giovanni. While passing the celebrations for a peasant wedding, he plans to amuse himself with the bride, Zerlina, before the wedding. He flirts with her in a delicious duet, "Là ci darem la mano" (Give me your hand). Flattered by these attentions from the great lord, she hesitates only a moment, then, picking up the melody, she embellishes and extends it. When he says "Andiam" (Let's go), she is by his side, and by the end of the duet is actually leading the way. Zerlina is prepared to play the game, first appearing shy and hesitant in the give and take of the verbal foreplay. Her brief resistance is titillating, encouraging, and grounded in good peasant common sense. Then, as she is drawn to the irresistible magnetism of the Don, she takes the lead. He simply extends his hand to her in a courteous gesture, with no pressure or force, and Zerlina takes his offered hand. This little seduction is all played out in the music.

But Zerlina, however aroused, can still listen to reason when Donna Elvira warns her of Don Giovanni's deceit. She thinks things through and decides not to risk believing the Don but to stay with Masetto, whom she loves. Later, in the ball scene, Don Giovanni dances with Zerlina one minute, then forcefully guides her into an adjoining room, where he would have raped her – but she screams, and her new husband, Masetto, comes to her rescue.

Leporello, sung by a bass, is Don Giovanni's servant; more, he is the Don's alter ego and shadow. At his master's side at all times, Leporello even becomes Don Giovanni on occasion – exchanging cloaks with him, flirting in his place, taking beatings on his behalf. One of Leporello's main functions is to keep track of his master's conquests – the Don is an obsessive collector of women, as interested in adding a new name to his list as in the conquest itself. In his brief aria "Fin ch'han dal vino" (Prepare a big feast until the wine makes all heads reel), Don Giovanni imagines an orgy at his ball, after which, "In the morning at least a dozen more names shall be added to the list." This is the list Leporello so cruelly recites to Donna Elvira, displaying a servant's pride in and identification with the power of his master.

Leporello is also Don Giovanni's scapegoat. More than that, suggests psychologist Otto Rank, "the servant is in fact identical with the master, but split off from him." Leporello is the Don's confidante in every love intrigue (after all, he keeps the books), and occasionally shares in his master's conquests. At the Don's bidding and disguised in his cape, Leporello flirts with and embraces Donna Elvira in the dark garden, leaving the Don free to serenade Elvira's maid at another window of the same house. When Don Giovanni is almost caught with Zerlina, he quickly puts his cloak and hat on Leporello, then pronounces his servant the guilty one when they are discovered. The assembled, outraged crowd grabs the Don to beat him, but are shocked to discover that they hold Leporello. Don Giovanni insults even his long-suffering servant when, on the way home from seducing Donna Elvira's maid, he claims to have seduced the valet's own girlfriend, a deed he laughingly recounts to the outraged Leporello, who, inextricably bound to his master, is even then unable to free himself from the Don's stronger personality.

Otto Rank suggests that "it would be impossible to create the Don Juan figure, the knight without conscience and without fear of death and the devil, if a part of him were not thereby split off into Leporello who represents the inner criticism, the anxiety, and the conscience of the hero." This being the case, it follows that "the enormity of Don Juan's wickedness is due to the splitting off of the inhibiting element of his personality." In some productions this close psychological connection is made very clear: the singers, (in one production brothers in real life), portray the roles of Don Giovanni and Leporello in such a way that it is often impossible to tell which is singing which role.

Donna Anna's father, the Commendatore, is a figure of divine retribution. He appears in the first scene just long enough to be killed by Don Giovanni. We next meet him, in Act II, as the statue in the cemetery, at whose feet the inscription reads "Here I await heaven's vengeance upon a vile assassin." Later, when he comes to dinner, he says, "Dammi la mano" (Give me your hand), echoing the line Don Giovanni used in so many seductions. When the constitutionally arrogant Don extends his hand, he is held in the statue's icy grip. But the Don, defiant to the last, refuses to repent. The statue drags him off to hell.

The tenor role of Don Ottavio, Donna Anna's fiancé, is one of the opera's less enviable characters. Throughout *Don Giovanni* he is held at arm's length by Anna, who demands that he support her in her grief, then tells him he must wait a year before they can be married – to all of which Ottavio agrees. He belongs in the realm of traditional *opera seria*; in that he has little interaction with characters other than Donna Anna, and little impact on the action. Mozart and da Ponte present him as an ineffective man, though he does have two glorious arias, both of them added following the first performance. In the first, "Dalla sua pace la mia dipende" (On her peace of mind depends mine too), he sings of his love for Donna Anna; in the second, "Il mio tesoro intanto andate a consolar" (Meantime go and console my dearest one), near the end of the opera, he asks his friends to console Anna while he goes to seek and kill the Don. Ottavio truly loves Donna Anna; theirs might have been a happy marriage had Anna not come in contact with the volatile Don. But, infected by Don Giovanni's energy, excitement, and passion, Anna is changed, stricken, no longer within the reach of the faithful Don Ottavio.

Masetto is a buffo character, a country boy whose fiancée the Don attempts to steal. He fights back the only way he knows – with violence – but is easily outwitted by the Don, who ends up beating him instead. In a touching duet, Masetto acts the betrayed husband as Zerlina coyly invites him to "Batti, batti" (Beat me, beat me, dear Masetto.

Punish your Zerlina. I am repentant). She clearly has Masetto wrapped around her little finger, and they soon kiss and make up.

Many people have reacted in many different ways to *Don Giovanni*. Kierkegaard, writing 50 years after the first performances and in love with Mozart's music, argues that the Don's existence is not verbal but musical, with such sensuous immediacy that what we are hearing is the life-force itself. "Mozart found a subject in Don Juan that is absolutely musical," Kierkegaard wrote. "Music takes place in time, it exists only in the moment of its performance." He defines Don Juan as constantly hovering between being an idea – that is, energy and the life-force itself – and being a real person. Don Juan is an image that constantly appears, Kierkegaard states, but does not take on form and substance. "He is an individual who is constantly being formed, but never finished." In music, Don Juan is a force of nature for whom the seduction of 2,065 women is not an impossibility, since he is an idea, not a man of flesh and blood. The number attached to the seductions is immaterial – Don Juan loves not one, but all. Faithful to none, he exists only in the moment. In desiring one woman, he desires all women. When Leporello suggests that he give up women, he laughs. "Give up women! You know very well I need women more than food and drink, or the very air I breathe!"

Today, Don Juan can be found in *The Rake's Progress*, by W.H. Auden and Chester Kallman, and set to music by Igor Stravinsky. The cynical, worldly-wise young rake cheats the devil and thus avoids death, but must spend the rest of his days in an insane asylum. Opera director Peter Sellars sets his film of *Don Giovanni* in the streets of any big U.S. city, in which the drinking and needle-pushing Don is interpreted as the leader of a street gang, self-serving and utterly remorseless. He enjoys the havoc he wreaks, beats Leporello, and laughs mockingly at the women he jilts.

Otto Rank, a colleague of Freud's, proposes an oedipal interpretation of the Don Juan character in which "the many seduced women represent the one unattainable mother, and the many men he deceives, fights, and kills represent the father. His constant striving and inability to love and remain with any one woman suggests he knows from the outset that each new conquest will fail him; the unattainable [mother] is beyond reach and all the while he is being consumed by a life of narcissistic excess." This Don Juan lives in the hell of his own desire.

This interpretation matches the thesis of a 20th-century opera, *Flammen*, composed by Erwin Schulhoff, in which Don Juan is condemned to never find peace or satisfaction. He sings, "Oh, to love once, then die." He longs for Death, La Morte – longs to make love to her. La Morte points to the stone statue: "Juan, don't you see how he pronounces eternal judgment on you – you are Juan, who can never die."

Our modern, secular age tends to demystify the Don Juan myth, removing the supernatural elements, downgrading the importance of the statue and the issues of hell-fire and divine retribution. Carlos Fuentes wrote a novel on the Don Juan theme, *Terra Nostra*, as recently as 1977. Roger Vailland wrote his novel, *Monsieur Jean*, in which the philandering Don is the managing director of a company who is killed when a heavy portrait falls on his head. The portrait is of his former assistant manager, Monsieur Commandeur. Today the Don is often described in psychoanalytic terms as aggressive, narcissistic, a man of obsessive behavior; his victims, Donna Anna and Elvira, are described as manic-depressive and masochistic.

There is both humor and irony in the fact that, in Mozart and da Ponte's telling of the tale, Don Giovanni, the macho lady-killer, has no success – he is figuratively impotent, foiled at every turn by Donna Anna, Donna Elvira, and Zerlina – all three. Conquest is only in his mind and in

Mozart's music, for even as the Don explored the realms of women, so Mozart ravished the realms of music. Don Giovanni and Mozart both flirted with many styles, both mixed with peasants and nobles on an equal basis, both spoke many languages, and conquered countless numbers of men and women, all of whom were and are in love with Mozart's music.

Two centuries after his death, Mozart continues to seduce us, defying the laws of time and space, for music exists only in the moment of performance. No wonder the spell of "Fin ch'han dal vino" is so mercurial – a vision as brief and sparkling as the bubbles in a glass of champagne – and vanishes when the music stops.

Characters

Don Giovanni	Baritone
Donna Anna, a noblewoman	Soprano
Don Ottavio, her fiancé	Tenor
The Commendatore, her father	Bass
Donna Elvira, Don Giovanni's abandoned wife	Soprano
Leporello, Don Giovanni's servant	Bass
Zerlina, a country girl	Soprano
Masetto, her fiancé	Bass

Bibliography
Benes, Karel and Brod, Max, *Flammen*, libretto, Decca/London 444 631-2, 1994.
Hoffman, E.T.A., "Don Juan," in *Tales from Hoffman*, Penguin Classics, 1990.
John, Nicholas, ed., *Don Giovanni*, English National Opera Guide 18, Riverrun Press Inc., New York, 1983.
Kierkegaard, Søren, "The Immediate Stages of the Erotic," in *Either/Or*, Princeton University Press, 1944.
Michener, James A., *Iberia*, Random House Inc., New York, 1968.
Miller, Jonathan, *Don Giovanni: Myths of Seduction and Betrayal*, Johns Hopkins University Press, Maryland, 1990.
Rank, Otto, *The Don Juan Legend*, Princeton University Press, 1975.

Agrippina

George Frideric Handel

Then Hendel strikes the Strings, the melting Strain
Transports the Soul, and thrills through ev'ry Vein.
– John Gay (1716)

Agrippina is one of the more colorful, sinister characters of Roman history. Driven by her ambition for her son, Nero, there were no lengths to which she would not go to have him named Emperor of Rome. After her brother, Caligula's, disastrous rule ended with his assassination, Claudius, their uncle, was proclaimed Emperor. Perceived as weak and simple, Claudius had always taken a back seat in family politics – no one had ever considered him a threat to the throne. Although he was partially paralyzed, stammered, limped, and slobbered, his mind was clear and brilliant. He played the fool, and his family left him alone to study and learn, to write histories and treatises.

When Caligula was assassinated in 41 A.D., Claudius was found trembling, hiding behind a curtain. He was brought forth by the Praetorian Guard and at once proclaimed Emperor by the Senate. Claudius turned out to be an intelligent, resourceful leader; Rome prospered under his rule, and, with the support of the army, the Empire grew. He appointed freedmen to key posts in every section of his administration; two of these, Narcissus and Pallas (both of whom appear in Handel's *Agrippina*), were appointed as his ministers of correspondence and accounts, respectively.

Claudius was eventually undone by his own dissipations – over-indulgence in sex, food, and alcohol – and by his wives. (He was described by a contemporary as "immoderate in his passion for women.") He divorced his first two wives, then married the teenage Messalina, who overnight acquired all the manners of an autocratic Empress. She took a series of lovers, and finally overstepped the mark when she publicly married a younger man. When news of this reached Claudius, he had the lover executed. A few days later, his soldiers appeared at Messalina's home and slaughtered her.

Claudius now needed another wife, and decided on Agrippina who, like him, was of the lineage of Caesar Augustus. The fact that Claudius and she were uncle and niece deterred neither; Claudius simply had the rules changed to allow the incestuous marriage. Agrippina had been married twice before; her first husband was Nero's father, and she poisoned her second. In marrying the older Emperor, Agrippina had one goal: to make Claudius agree to name Nero as his heir. In the five years of their marriage, she achieved just that. Claudius adopted Nero and named him his successor, putting aside his own son, Brittanicus. He also married his young daughter Octavia to Nero, thus consolidating the line of succession.

In 54 A.D., when Agrippina realized that Claudius was becoming aware of her lust for power, she poisoned him. History relates the story of his death: Because the Emperor employed tasters to ensure that his food was not contaminated, Agrippina had to find another way to administer the deadly poison. One night at a banquet, she arranged that she would be served a plate of special mushrooms that Claudius loved. She fed the mushrooms to her husband one by one; death followed hours later. The Senate declared Claudius a god, and Nero became Emperor at 17 years of age, his mother ruling by his side. It is said that Nero remarked at the time, "Mushrooms must be food for the gods, since by eating them Claudius has become divine."

Agrippina's victory was not to last. Five years after becoming Emperor, Nero, tired of his controlling mother and encouraged by his second wife, Poppea, had Agrippina killed. He first arranged for the sinking of a fabulous ship on which his mother was to sail in the Bay of Naples, but Agrippina survived the shipwreck by swimming ashore. Days later, Nero sent his soldiers to kill her at her country house.

Thus runs the horror story of the Caesars in the early years of Christianity. Most of these historically scheming characters appear in the opera: Agrippina and her teenage son, Nerone (Nero); Claudio (Claudius), her uncle, husband, and Emperor; Pallante (Pallas) and Narciso (Narcissus), ministers of her husband and both in love with Agrippina; and Poppea, who is loved by Claudio, Nerone, and the general Ottone (Otho).

The excellent libretto was written especially for Handel by a distinguished diplomat, Cardinal Grimani, whose text blends serious emotions and comic situations with an overriding sense of irony. Grimani took as his sources the *Annals* of Tacitus and Suetonius's *Lives of the Caesars*. His libretto was generally viewed as a satire on the Papal court of his day; as such, the plot of his anti-heroic comedy was highly popular with the audiences of 18th-century Italy.

The opera begins with Agrippina telling her son, Nerone, that she has received a letter informing her that her husband, the Emperor Claudio, has died in a storm at sea while returning home from his campaign in Britain. Agrippina plots at once with the freedmen Narciso and Pallante to have Nerone proclaimed Emperor. But just as Nerone and Agrippina are ascending the throne, news comes that Claudio is alive, saved from drowning by his general, Ottone. The chastened Agrippina steps down, pretending to be delighted at her husband's safe return. Underneath, however, she is seething, and more determined than ever to put Nerone on the throne. To achieve this end, she sets in motion the wheels of an intricate plot. She approaches Poppea and tells her that her lover, Ottone, has betrayed her, preferring to take Claudio's offer of the throne and ceding Poppea to Claudio in exchange. Furious, Poppea speaks with Claudio as soon as he returns, and cajoles him into agreeing to have Ottone removed from the succession. He quickly agrees to demote Ottone in exchange for Poppea's love – a ruse on her part, for she keeps Claudio at a distance throughout the opera.

Act II opens with the celebration of Claudio's victory in Britain. Ottone, unaware of the forces moving against him, is thunderstruck when Claudio denounces him as a traitor. Amazed to find himself rejected and curtly dismissed by Agrippina, Nerone, and even Poppea for saving Claudio's life, Ottone is confused and unhappy. Left alone, accompanied only by a mournful oboe, Ottone sings "Voi che udite il mio lamento" (You who hear my complaint) directly to the audience, to music that describes his utter despair. He and Poppea later make up when they realize that Agrippina is the cause of the intrigue against him.

Agrippina now enters, concerned that her plotting is getting out of control. She gives full rein to her conspiring imagination in an extended *scena* that begins with a demand to the gods to let her son rule. In a fast middle section, "Quel ch'oprai è soggetto a gran periglio" (The scheme I labor for lies in great peril), she ponders the danger in which she finds herself. Pallante and Narciso know too much, she thinks, and Ottone must be eliminated to make way for Nerone. Pallante enters and assures Agrippina of his loyalty. She tells him she wants him to kill Ottone and Narciso because they are her enemies. Pallante agrees to do her will and leaves. Narciso then arrives, and Agrippina asks him to kill Pallante and Ottone. For love of Agrippina, he also agrees.

Claudio enters, greeting his wife with "I come to gaze, my sweet, on those rays of love from your beautiful eyes." The irony is obvious – Claudio can't wait to leave Agrippina to go to Poppea. In a long, manipulative dialogue, Agrippina convinces her husband that Ottone plans his downfall and must be "Plucked like a poisonous root out of the ground." Claudio wonders whom he could trust if Ottone is demoted, "For jealousy is the companion of authority." Agrippina proposes Nerone, assuring her husband that "His respect for me, his mother, will make his heart submissive to you, as a father." Claudio wants time to think this over, but Agrippina insists. At this moment, Lesbo, a servant, arrives to tell Claudio, in an aside, that Poppea awaits him. Impatient to go, Claudio grants Agrippina her wish: Nerone shall be his heir. With that he rushes off, leaving the triumphant Agrippina alone onstage to end the act in a wonderful dance-like aria, "Fate smiles favorably on me today."

Act III opens with a farcical scene in Poppea's bedroom in which all three of her would-be lovers traipse through in succession. First Ottone appears; Poppea tells him she loves him, but he must hide and ignore whatever he hears. Then the impetuous Nerone arrives; Poppea tells him she loves him, but he is late and so must hide because she is expecting Agrippina. Next Claudio shows up; Poppea tells him it is Nerone, not Ottone, who seeks her favors. Nerone, thinking Claudio has gone, emerges from behind a curtain only to face the fury of his stepfather, who denounces him. Before Claudio leaves, Poppea asks for his protection. Poppea, at last alone with her third hidden lover, Ottone, insists that she loves only him. This farcical bedroom scene was to be repeated years later by Mozart, in the opening scene of *The*

Marriage of Figaro.

Nerone goes straight to Agrippina, who demands that he give up all thoughts of Poppea. He agrees. Meanwhile, Claudio, totally confused as to who is telling the truth, complains, "Agrippina, Nerone, Ottone, Poppea trouble my peace of mind in accusing one another. Nor do I know who is telling the truth and who lying." In an attempt to unravel the confusion, he calls all the leading protagonists together. He announces that Poppea is to be given in marriage to Nerone, and appoints Ottone as his successor. No one is happy with this decision. Ottone refuses the throne – he will not give Poppea up – so Claudio instead gives Poppea to Ottone, the man she really loves, and names Nerone as his heir, which appeases the ruthless Agrippina. The goddess Giunone (Juno) arrives to bless the happy resolution as the curtain falls.

With this ending, Handel and Grimani rearranged the historical facts somewhat, and stopped short of Agrippina's poisoning of Claudio. But that's material for an unwritten sequel, *Agrippina Part 2.*

The two women in the opera, Agrippina and Poppea, both roles written for sopranos, are brilliantly contrasted: one is unscrupulous and scheming, the other happy-go-lucky and fickle. Agrippina dominates the opera in the first two acts, confident of her power in "L'alma mia" (My soul), and more than a little menacing in "Tu ben degno" (Worthy are you), an aria in which her suppressed violence and passion are referred to in the bass. She begins her famous Act II *scena* with a long, winding melody accompanied by a solo oboe, with comments from the violins in *ritornellos*, or recurring phrases. Her final aria of the *scena* is exuberant as she anticipates success, the rhythm of her music seductive and waltz-like – almost foot-tappingly so. In her only aria in Act III, "Si voi pace" (If you want peace), she assures Claudio of her love and loyalty in music that is again set to seductive dance rhythms.

In contrast, Poppea's main concern throughout the opera is with enjoying life to the full and trying to keep straight the intrigues of her three suitors; Handel consistently paints her moods in colors that are bright, happy, and infectious. We first meet her sitting before her mirror, adorning herself. Her music is gay and bright: "Precious jewels and flowers," she sings, "increase the rarity of my beauty." She sings a total of nine short arias in the opera, all of them melodious and light, regardless of whether she is longing for love, angry at a lover, or admiring her reflection. She is the prototype of the titular character of *Semele* (an opera Handel composed years later) – a lively, likable, exuberant young woman, used by Agrippina but sincerely in love with Ottone. Her final aria, "Bel piacer" (To enjoy faithful love), with its changing rhythms and catchy melody, reaffirms her teasing, affectionate character.

Nerone, an untidy boy, unschooled in everything but his mother's evil ways, is a teenager in the opera, not yet the monster he was destined to become. Originally written for a soprano castrato, today this role can be sung by a mezzo-soprano or countertenor. The style is florid, with much coloratura and embellishment of the vocal line; the catchy rhythms and changing harmonies of Nerone's arias reflect his mercurial nature. He vacillates easily. He first tells Poppea, "My love is already quite ravenous for its satisfaction." Later, when his mother tells him to cast Poppea out of his heart, he responds, "Come nube che fugge" (As a cloud flies from the wind I renounce her despised face) in a brief, brilliant, bravura aria with no fewer than six instrumental solos. One is not entirely convinced by Nerone's plan to give up Poppea; after divorcing Octavia, the historical Nero married Poppea and, at her urging, murdered his mother.

Ottone, written for a contralto, may be sung today by a countertenor. Ottone is the only honest and truly tragic character in the opera (and in history), and as such acts as a foil to the rest of the cast. His Act I aria, "Lusinghiera mia speranza" (O flattering hope), expresses his happiness on his return from the military campaign and his anticipation of being reunited with Poppea, but the music – in its agitation, intricate rhythms, and interrupted cadences – suggests that all is not well. In Ottone's arias, the words frequently pull against the music, describing one thought or emotion even as the music expresses something quite different. As an example, in Ottone's Act II aria "Coronato il crin d'alloro" (I will be crowned with the laurel wreath), he sings in a mood more reflective than jubilant as he weighs his choices in a cross-current of emotions until, finally, he decides to give up the throne in favor of Poppea: "Greater still is my desire for the beauty I adore."

The Emperor Claudio is sung by a bass. (Tenors rarely sang leading roles in baroque operas, which depended on the brilliance of soprano and castrato stars for fame and success.) As was the historical Claudius, Claudio is presented as a victim of his passions, of his wife Agrippina, and of the woman he desires, Poppea. Unpredictable and vain one moment, amorous the next, he is manipulated by both women when, for different reasons, they demand that Ottone not be named successor to the throne. He is further manipulated by Poppea when his stepson, Nerone, appears in Poppea's bedroom. Frustrated and uncomprehending, the great Roman Emperor flounders. His indecisiveness and physical clumsiness are suggested in his music by vocal leaps and bounds, yet Handel gives Claudio one of the loveliest numbers in the entire opera, an arietta sung to Poppea: "Vieni, o caro" (Come, O dearest), as tender a love song as is found anywhere in opera, baroque or otherwise.

Narciso and Pallante, the two freedmen, are differentiated by vocal pitch: Pallante is a blundering bass, Narciso a plaintive alto. This comic pair love the same woman, plot together, and are made fools of together – a kind of Roman

Laurel and Hardy.

These operatic characters conform to conventions of the baroque period which are rarely found in opera today. One convention that most clearly defines the era is the crossover of roles in terms of gender: Men sing women's roles, and vice versa. In The Santa Fe Opera's production of *Agrippina*, Nerone is sung by a mezzo-soprano in place of the original castrato. The first castratos sang in churches in the mid-16th century. With the emergence of the castrato in the early 17th century, Italy began a tradition that changed the course of opera, making it a dynamic and highly popular form of entertainment. Worshiped like gods, castratos were greatly responsible for the enormous popularity of Italian opera well into the 19th century. Writers of the time reported that these singers displayed extraordinary skill in bravura singing, trills, scales, and vocal leaps and jumps, all with a unique, high, pure sound with a timbre all its own. They had amazing breath control and, with their uncannily beautiful sound, were capable of expressing noble sentiments with great pathos in the *opera seria* of their day. Castratos demanded – and received – exorbitant fees and superstar treatment. One such singer demanded that he should always enter on horseback, wearing a helmet of six-foot-tall multicolored plumes, and singing the same entrance aria, regardless of the opera being performed. The inclusion of arias that were personal favorites of the singers, whether the aria fit the opera at hand or not, was common practice.

Today, countertenors often sing roles originally composed for castratos. The high male voice of the countertenor has a range a fifth higher than a tenor, and is not unlike an alto sound. (It is still not clear whether the countertenor uses falsetto or is an extended tenor.) The roles of Ottone and Narciso, originally composed for contralto and alto castratos, are sung today by countertenors. Nerone, originally a soprano castrato, may be sung by either a countertenor or a mezzo-soprano.

The borrowing, by composers, of music from one opera and placing it in another was another convention of the baroque; Handel borrowed from himself all the time. He was able to compose *Agrippina* (and many subsequent operas) in a very short space of time because many of the arias had already appeared in earlier cantatas or oratorios. Only five of *Agrippina*'s more than 40 musical sections were originally written for this opera; the remainder had been previously composed and performed. One of *Agrippina*'s first arias, "Ho un non so nel cor" (There is something in my heart), a bouncy piece in which she exults in her devious powers, was originally composed for *La Resurrezione*, in which Mary Magdalene, on her way to heaven, looks forward to the resurrection – singing the same music! This 18th-century convention of borrowing is entirely alien to us today.

Italian opera audiences of the 17th and 18th centuries, reared on commedia dell'arte, loved comedy and caricature, which became major components of baroque opera. Scenes with magnificent sets, costumes, and lighting effects were presented in quick succession. Amazing spectacles became a major feature, with special machines providing breathtaking effects of gods descending, ghostly appearances, battles, oracles, and dreams. Audiences witnessed miraculous and supernatural events on a enormous scale.

Agrippina was composed during the early years of Handel's career, toward the end of his Italian period (1706–1709). The score is rich and varied in melody, harmony, and rhythm. Handel makes the two major components of baroque opera flow easily: the recitatives, which are the conversational sections that advance the plot and link the arias with only minimal accompaniment; and the da capo arias. He uses the orchestra ingeniously in both; listen for the continuo, the bass accompaniment to the recitatives, to which he sometimes added one or two instruments. In a da capo aria, the first section is followed by a contrasting section, often in another key, then by a return to the head (i.e., *da capo*) of the first section, usually with ornamentation on the repeat. This A-B-A form was a perfect way to show off a singer's virtuosity, since it gave the singer the freedom to embellish and ornament at will in the repeated section.

The da capo aria became Handel's primary dramatic medium; he found numerous ways in which to vary, experiment with, and explore the form to make it more exciting and expressive. Obbligato instrumental solos appear in many arias, adding richness, color, and depth to the emotions expressed, the instruments equal partners with the voice. The full orchestra plays recurring themes, or *ritornellos*, and Handel frequently introduces full orchestral interludes between the sung sections. His orchestra was made up mainly of stringed and wind instruments; horns and trumpets, were reserved for the chorus, and for ceremonial or special effects. Because Handel usually played the cembalo (harpsichord) himself in performance, his improvisations are rarely marked in the score – a great loss to the musicians who followed him.

The essence of Handel's style is not to present characters as "real" people, as we tend to do today, but rather as personifications of passions, as the idealizations of emotions. Baroque composers deliberately sought to create mood, to interpret the feelings, thoughts, and hidden motivations of their characters, rather than delineating them primarily through their actions. This is key to understanding the baroque style and its composers, especially Handel. As musicologist Hugo Leichtentritt says in Grout's *A Short History of Opera*, characters in baroque opera "at any given moment of expression are, for the time being, simply the incarnation of a certain state of mind and feeling, thus the complete character is obtained by the synthesis of all these expressive moments rather than, as in modern drama, by the analysis of complex moods expressed in a single aria or scene." This is what Handel so magnificently achieves in his operas. Handel, born in Halle in 1685 (the same year as J.S. Bach), determined to play music from an early age. By the age of 17, he had already excelled as the organist at the Calvinist cathedral. Following his father's death, he moved to Hamburg, a city with its own public opera house, and the center of German opera, or *opera seria*, as it was called. Here he learned and fell in love with opera under Reinhard Keiser, a brilliant composer who crafted his works in the Italian style, with some refinements of his own. Keiser was an enormous influence on the young Handel, who often "borrowed" his mentor's music for his own operas, much to Keiser's chagrin. Handel's first opera, *Almira*, was performed in Hamburg in 1705; he was 19 years old.

The following year Handel traveled to Italy, where he was to spend nearly four years, traveling and immersing himself in the Italian style by attending operas in the theatres, cantatas and oratorios in princely palaces, and sacred music in churches. He met and made friends with the nobility, the court, princes of the Church, and the leading composers of his day, including Alessandro Scarlatti and his son, Domenico. Nicknamed "Il Sassone" (The Saxon) by the Italians, the kindly if somewhat rough-mannered young musician came to love Italy, and was respected by everyone he met.

Handel was employed in the household of the Marquess Ruspoli and appointed chamber musician to two influential Cardinals, Pamphili and Ottoboni, for whom he composed weekly chamber cantatas, church compositions, and large-scale cantatas for special occasions. In these years there was little difference between the cantata, the opera, and the oratorio; all three forms included *recitative secco* and da capo arias with intense emotional expression. Handel viewed these early compositions as his training ground for opera and for mastering the Italian language and style. He was to use and rework virtually all of these early compositions in his two "Italian" operas, *Rodrigo* and *Agrippina*, as well as in later works.

In 1709, Handel rapidly composed the comedic *Agrippina* for the Venetian winter carnival season. The opera's premiere was held in the theatre of Cardinal Grimani's family, the Teatro di San Giovanni Crisostomo, and was an enormous success. The Venetians loved the cynicism, irony, and black comedy of this new work based loosely on ancient Roman history. Grimani managed to find a fine balance between a comic interpretation and a passionate, even tragic, one – the tone of the dialogue may be bantering, but Handel's arias express true feeling. The characters are never caricatures, but are treated compassionately and humanely, regardless of their transgressions. Handel's light treatment of his grim historical subject directly influenced the *buffo* operas of later composers such as Mozart, Rossini, and Donizetti.

The key to the success of any 21st-century production of *Agrippina* is how well the singers interpret the mood music of the baroque characters they portray, and how well the director provides comedy and pathos, maintaining the balance between farce and comedy. The complex plot of *Agrippina* becomes quite clear in the theatre; the human qualities of the characters are convincing, and the dialogue flows easily and comprehensibly in both Italian and supertitles. The story unfolds smoothly as the characters develop out of their arias advancing the plot. *Agrippina* is a musical feast by any standard, and Handel's characterizations give the work its strength as one of the most brilliant operas of the baroque era.

♪

Characters

Claudio, Emperor of Rome	Bass
Agrippina, his wife	Soprano
Nerone, her son	Mezzo-soprano (soprano castrato)
Poppea, a Roman woman	Soprano
Ottone, a Roman general	Countertenor (contralto castrato)
Pallante, a Roman minister	Bass
Narciso, a Roman minister	Countertenor (alto castrato)

Bibliography

Dean, W. and J.M. Knapp, *Handel's Operas 1704–1726*, Clarendon Press, Oxford, 1995.

Durant, Will, *Caesar and Christ: The Story of Civilization: Part III*, Simon and Schuster, New York, 1944.

Grout, Donald Jay, *A Short History of Opera*, Columbia University Press, New York, 1965.

Hogwood, Christopher, *Handel*, Thames and Hudson, New York, 1988.

Sadie, Stanley, ed., *The Grove Dictionary of Opera*, Vol. II, MacMillan Reference Ltd., London, 1998.

Schmidgall, Gary, *Literature as Opera*, Oxford University Press, Oxford, 1980.

Schoenberg, Harold C., *The Lives of the Great Composers*, W.W. Norton & Co., New York, 1981.

Suetonius, Vol. II, *Lives of the Caesars*, Harvard University Press, 1997.

La Sonnambula

Vincenzo Bellini

Dreaming sleepwalkers surmount obstacles with the song of the unconscious. – Catherine Clément

In the failing dusk, a window of the mill-house opens high above the ground. A mysterious white figure appears to float out of the casement window. It walks slowly, deliberately along the ledge of the roof, toward the plank bridge that passes above the churning mill wheel. The crowd below gasps at the appearance of this *fantasma* (phantom). The slender figure – a young woman – seems to hover over the rotten boards beneath her feet, her gaze fixed, her nightgown trailing behind her and moving gently in the cool night air, her dark hair flowing down her back. The crowd, knowing the danger, is transfixed; one misstep and the girl will plunge to her death in the great mill wheel and its rush of water. Even the music holds back, lest an unexpected sound throw her off balance. Held in the arms of protective sleep, she freely gives voice to all that is in her heart. Suddenly, the crowd recognizes Amina, a young girl of the village, whom they all love. As the sleeping Amina walks, caught between death in the darkness below and a magical, enchanted sleep, she sings in blind ecstasy of her love and longing for her fiancé, Elvino, and of their mystical union, her voice soaring beyond earth, time, and space. Alone in her passion, beyond reach, she carries us with her.

Opera demands this of its heroines. The ordeals must be endured and they must pass the tests – singing. They must cross bridges and confront their fears in order to reach the safety of the other side. They do not all return to life – Tosca chooses death as she jumps from the parapet of the Castel' Sant' Angelo, Brünnhilde chooses the fire and union in death with her beloved, and Isolde simply dies "as if transfigured," (according to Wagner's final stage direction for her.) Amina, however, returns both herself and us to time and reality when, having crossed the high bridge, she feels the earth beneath her feet at a safe distance from the yawning jaws of the mill wheel. She wakes to the world of men to find not death, but life in which her engagement ring is returned to her finger, her beloved kneeling at her feet, and her mother's arms enfolding her. Dazed and confused, still half in that other world into which her voice and song carried her, she sings of transforming the world into a paradise of love.

This is the ultimate scene of Vincenzo Bellini's *La Sonnambula* (The Sleepwalker). Little was known about somnambulism in the early 19th century; the villagers of the small Swiss hamlet in which the opera is set were ignorant of such phenomena. Superstitiously, they speak in hushed tones of a roaming phantom: "At dead of night a shade descends from the hill, clad in white attire with flowing locks and eyes of fire, like a thick mist stirred by the wind. It advances, grows, becomes immense. No leaf stirs, nothing breathes, even the dogs, crouched on the ground, make no sound." Afraid of what they don't understand, their imaginations run wild, and they infect one another with their fear.

The story of the opera is as simple as a fairytale. High

in the Swiss Alps, in a little village, lives a pretty young girl named Amina. She is an orphan who has been raised by Teresa, the mill owner, who loves Amina as her own daughter. Amina is engaged to Elvino, a prosperous young farmer who is the catch of the town. He is also loved by Lisa, the keeper of the village inn. Elvino and Lisa had once been a couple, but he cast her off in favor of Amina. Ever since, Lisa has resented her rival. Her opportunity for revenge comes when an unknown stranger arrives in town and spends a night at her inn.

In the opening scene, the villagers celebrate the betrothal of Elvino and Amina, who shyly expresses her happiness. Elvino appears, having just visited the grave of his mother to seek her blessing. As his token of love and betrothal, he places his mother's ring on Amina's finger. The festivities are interrupted by the arrival of a stranger, Rodolfo, who asks the way to the castle. Lisa assures him that it is too late to reach the castle before dark and invites him to spend the night at the inn. Rodolfo, who from his bearing and manner is clearly a Lord, asks about the old Count, and is told he died some years before and that his heir has disappeared.

Rodolfo appears to know the village. He casts admiring glances at Amina, tells her she reminds him of a young woman once dear to him, and bids her goodnight with "I hope your husband will love you as I would." The volatile Elvino is annoyed by the compliments this stranger pays his fiancée. The sounds of shepherds' pipes are heard as they return with their flocks from the hills, a touch not to be missed in this pastoral melodrama. Lisa suggests that they all retire before the *fantasma* appears, but Rodolfo, an educated man, laughs at their superstitions. "This image has been conjured up by your own blind credulity," he assures them as he goes to his room. "The time will come when the village will be rid of such apparitions." Left alone, Elvino accuses Amina of flirting with the stranger, but she convinces him she loves only him; the scene ends with their love duet.

In scene ii, at the inn, Lisa knocks at Rodolfo's door and is invited to enter. She has learned that he is the son of their beloved Count. Rodolfo admits that this is true, and is flirting with the pretty innkeeper when they are interrupted by a sound from the window. Lisa runs to hide, not wanting to be found in Rodolfo's room; she leaves moments later, but not before catching sight of Amina at the window. In Lisa's haste to leave, she drops her scarf. The window opens, and Amina, wearing a simple white nightdress, enters the room. The bemused Rodolfo realizes at once that this is no nocturnal phantom but the sleepwalking Amina.

Given the mores of the period (the opera premiered in 1831), this would be a tricky moment for Amina, were she awake – alone in the bedroom of a nobleman who clearly finds her attractive. This thought crosses Rodolfo's mind as he approaches her, intending to embrace the sleeping girl. She reaches out to him, believing, in her sleep, that he is Elvino and that they are on their way to church to be wed. But Rodolfo stops himself – "What am I doing?" He decides to leave Amina in his room; he will sleep in another. The oblivious Amina sings of eternal fidelity and love, then sinks onto the sofa and drops into a deep, normal sleep.

The next morning, when the villagers come to the inn to pay their respects to their new Lord, they are amazed to find the door to his room open, the Count gone, and Amina sleeping on the sofa. They assume the worst. Lisa bursts in, followed by Elvino. She has told him what he would find, but he doesn't believe her until he sees the sleeping Amina. As she wakens, confused and wondering where she is, Elvino accuses her of betrayal and, in an exciting ensemble, breaks off their engagement – to the delight of Lisa, the confusion of the villagers, and the anger of Teresa, who defends her daughter. The village's pastoral happiness is temporarily disrupted, the wedding is off, and Amina collapses in tears.

When Act II begins, the villagers have partially returned to their senses. They decide to ask the new Count about what happened, fully confident that he will confirm Amina's innocence. Amina meets Elvino, who continues to cruelly accuse her of betrayal. Caught up in his own suffering, he refuses to listen to her heartfelt pleas. The returning villagers joyfully tell Elvino that the Count has confirmed Amina's virtue and innocence, but Elvino does not believe them; insinuating that the Count is a liar, he tears his mother's ring from Amina's hand.

The pace of the opera quickens: Lisa, the cause of all the chaos, hears the villagers announcing that Elvino has decided to marry her that very day; when Elvino appears, she forgives him and agrees to marry him. Rodolfo then appears and attempts to explain to Elvino that Amina was sleepwalking, but Elvino says he is making it up. The argument escalates until Teresa calls for quiet from the mill-house window, explaining that Amina has fallen into an exhausted sleep. She is horrified to learn that Elvino is about to marry Lisa. "I don't think so," she says, producing Lisa's scarf, which she had picked up in the Count's room early that morning. Lisa cannot deny it. The dumbfounded Elvino cries out, "Lisa, guilty of the self-same fault? Love is no more, no faith, no honor!" He asks if anyone can prove Amina's innocence. Rodolfo catches his arm and points to the window above the mill wheel. "She herself," he answers.

The breathless crowd watches the sleeping Amina step out of the mill window and walk along the narrow ledge of the roof. One slip and she will fall to her death. They watch as she gradually makes her way across the roof, singing all the while of her love for Elvino. She nearly falls when a broken board gives way beneath her feet, but recovers her balance and walks on to safety. Bellini and his librettist, Felice Romani, well understood that this high-wire act, overlaid with the etheric singing of the sleepwalking girl, would be riveting. Rodolfo holds Elvino back until Amina reaches safety, then runs to her, returns his mother's ring to her finger, and, as she awakens, embraces her. As the village's collective adrenaline returns to normal, Elvino leads his Amina to church in a classic happy-ever-after ending. The greatness of *La Sonnambula* lies not in its simple, sympathetic story but in its music and its singers. "Melody, melody, melody," is what Niccolò Antonio Zingarelli, one of the last great composers of *opera seria* and Bellini's teacher, drummed into him. Bellini moved away from the repeats and recapitulations that were integral parts of the da capo style. A contemporary reviewer, Domenico de Paoli describes Bellini's technique well: "The melody begins and develops without ever returning upon itself: each note appears to rise from the preceding one like a fruit from a flower, always new, always unforeseen, always logical, and concludes without a single recall of any one of its phrases." Richard Wagner respected Bellini for just these attributes; his second opera, *Das Liebesverbot*, was consciously modeled on Bellini's works.

Bellini's operas have been described as *Liederspiel* (song-plays) because each situation is encapsulated in its own well-rounded compact song. Nowhere is this truer than in *La Sonnambula*, which is a series of charming, beautiful songs. The German composer, Ferdinand Hiller, writing as quoted in Weinstock's *Vincenzo Bellini*, asks, "What was it then that gave this muse such quick and almost universal recognition? In combination with his sensuous appeal, it was the sincerity of his emotion and the simplicity with which he expressed himself." Bellini's compositions were always about the singing, first and foremost; he paid little attention to orchestration. Giuseppe Verdi acknowledged Bellini's poor orchestration but also said that Bellini's music "is rich in feeling. In his operas there are long, long, long melodies such as no one before him produced." Chopin was also deeply influenced by the romantic Bellini.

La Sonnambula requires outstanding singers whose coloratura voices can soar effortlessly and who can thrill with the sheer beauty of their sound, for this is bel canto opera at its best. Bel canto refers to the graceful style of singing in the 18th and early 19th centuries. Rossini's concept of a bel canto singer involved three requirements: a naturally beautiful voice, even in tone; careful training that encouraged effortless delivery of highly florid music; and a mastery of style that was assimilated from listening to the best Italian exponents. A coloratura role in the bel canto style is one in which the singer, usually a soprano, has a flexibility and range that permits seemingly effortless ornamentation of the vocal line while maintaining sweetness of tone and purity of timbre.

Since its premiere in 1831, *La Sonnambula* has been a showcase work for great sopranos, from Giuditta Pasta, who created the role, to Jenny Lind, Adelina Patti, Maria Callas, and Joan Sutherland. The tradition continues with the extraordinary French soprano Natalie Dessay, who sings Amina in The Santa Fe Opera's production.

La Sonnambula does not belong entirely to the soprano, however. The tenor and bass roles of Elvino and Rodolfo, respectively, hold their own with the soprano in some of the loveliest music Bellini composed for male singers. The chorus of villagers also fills an important role, beginning with their "Viva, viva, Amina" (Act I, scene i), to the accompaniment of an onstage *banda*. As the plot progresses, the villagers prove to be fickle, superstitious, and easily swayed, as their allegiance shifts from Amina to Lisa and back to Amina. Such is human nature.

Amina's opening aria, "Come per me sereno" (How bright this day), is exquisite for its melodic beauty and depiction of her sweet, simple, trusting nature; at once we are introduced to the brilliance of the soprano's coloratura in the cabaletta – the fast, final section of the aria. Elvino's aria "Prendi: l'anel ti dono" (Accept this ring I give you) describes the exuberance of the amorous, ardent tenor in music that requires no fewer than four top Cs in the cabaletta. The elegant, educated Rodolfo provides a rational, if flirtatious, base that anchors the story's flights of fancy.

La Sonnambula was a departure for Bellini; his earlier operas *Il Pirata* and *I Capuleti e i Montecchi*, and the later *Norma* and *I Puritani*, dealt with plots of historical intensity with much more dramatic substance. *La Sonnambula* came about almost by accident. Bellini and librettist Felice Romani, with whom he collaborated on most of his major operas, had planned to compose *Ernani* for Milan's Carnival season in the winter of 1830–31, but they dropped the project at the last moment because they were afraid of censorship given the political nature of the subject matter. Romani was busy that season writing the libretto for Donizetti's *Anna Bolena*, which premiered in the same theatre that same season. Soprano Giuditta Pasta premiered the roles of both Anna Bolena and Amina.

Romani and Bellini took as their source for *La Sonnambula* a short work by Eugène Scribe, the elegance of whose writing fit well with Romani's romantic style. The collaboration proceeded fairly smoothly but for one major bone of contention. Romani suggested that Rodolfo, on seeing and admiring Amina in Act I, should be revealed later as her father. After all, Romani argued, in both his own libretto and Scribe's original, Rodolfo is clearly familiar with the village, and says to Amina, "You do not know how sweetly those lovely eyes touch my heart nor what memories they stir of a beauty I adored. She was just like you." If Rodolfo had had an affair in the village years earlier and perhaps had left because of it, the orphaned Amina could conceivably be his daughter. This makes dramatic sense; otherwise, why is Rodolfo so taken with Amina, a stranger who merely reminds him of someone he once knew? Bellini, however, refused to consider the proposal.

Bellini began composing *La Sonnambula* early in January 1831. Unlike the other two great composers of bel canto opera, Rossini and Donizetti, Bellini did not like to compose rapidly, or meet short deadlines as they did, but in this case he had no choice – the premiere was scheduled for the following month. Not too far behind schedule, *La Sonnambula* was presented on March 6 in Milan's Teatro Carcano and was a major success on all fronts – for the composer, for the librettist, and for soprano Giuditta Pasta and her Elvino, tenor Giovanni Rubini, two singers for whom Bellini composed many principal roles.

Bellini shaped the principal roles of each opera to the singers who would first interpret them. He also believed, contrary to common practice, that singers should sing in character rather than merely sounding beautiful. He wanted shifting emotions and individual characteristics expressed in both acting and singing. When he first met Rubini in rehearsals for *Il Pirata*, there were problems; Rubini sang beautifully, but with no sense of character. Finally, Bellini burst out, "You don't put half the spirit you have into it. When you should be driving the audience out of its mind, you are cold and languishing. Show your passion – haven't you ever been in love?" Rubini, confused, just stood there. Bellini explained, "I want to introduce a new kind of music which expresses the words very closely. You can do it." To demonstrate what he meant, Bellini began to sing. "His voice had no special quality," reported Filippo Cicconetti, one of Bellini's biographers, "but his face and body were so animated and brought so much fire that it would have torn apart the hardest of men." Suddenly, Bellini was joined by Rubini's glorious voice. He now understood what was required of him, and went on to become the tenor Bellini most treasured.

Born in Catania, Sicily, Vincenzo Bellini showed early promise in music and was sent to study at age 18 at the Naples Conservatory. His graduation work, an opera called *Adelson e Salvini*, was so successful that he was commissioned out of college to compose an opera for the Teatro San Carlo. The resulting work, *Il Pirata*, brought the young composer to the attention of the great opera houses. Bellini joined Rossini and Donizetti in creating a period of opera in which bel canto or beautiful singing was the primary goal. Bellini respected and revered Rossini, whose work he emulated; he was at first friendly with Donizetti, but later grew jealous of him and saw him as a rival. The paths of the three men crossed and re-crossed many times in the course of their careers, and at last brought all three of them to Paris, where spent their final years.

Heinrich Heine, the great German poet, described Bellini: "He was tall, slenderly built, moved gracefully, always self-consciously. He had light blond, almost golden hair combed into thin little curls and dressed in such a romantically wistful fashion. His clothes fitted his fragile figure so caressingly and he carried his little Malacca cane in such an idyllic manner he always reminded me of the young shepherds in our pastoral plays. There was something vague, an absence of character in his features; his face expressed sorrow without depth. His gait was so elegiac and ethereal. In every respect the man looked like a sigh in dancing pumps." This none too kind description is the personification of the romantic hero, melancholic and doomed – one who could not be long for this world. Bellini was both attracted to and repelled by Heine, who, in his own words, predicted Bellini's early death: "I prophesied jokingly that in his capacity as a genius he would die soon." The young composer avoided Heine after that, calling him the "possessor of the evil eye." However weeks later, in 1835, Bellini died in Paris of liver and intestinal complications at the age of 34.

A Note on Somnambulism

Everyone is familiar with the phenomenon of somnambulism, or sleepwalking. Many people know of family members or friends who get up and wander about at night in their sleep; statistically, 18% of the population is prone to sleepwalking. Little was understood about this anomaly in Bellini's time, and not much more is known today. Not considered an illness per se, sleepwalking seems to occur randomly and infrequently. Often triggered by fatigue or anxiety, it usually occurs early in the night during non-REM sleep and can last from a few seconds to more than half an hour.

The sleepwalker, with wide-open eyes and blank stare, can move about; the brain converts actual objects in the sleepwalker's path into dream-state analogs, thus enabling the sleepwalker to circumvent them. The sleepwalker speaks in a mumbling, slurred fashion, can dress, undress, go to the bathroom, eat, switch lights on and off, and open, close, and even unlock doors – all while asleep. The danger lies in objects the sleepwalker may not "see;" beyond this, the sleepwalker seems almost protected, and usually comes to no harm.

Somnambulists sleep deeply while walking, and are usually difficult to awaken. Left alone, they will find their way back to bed or to some place where they can lie down to resume normal sleep. With a little calm encouragement and guidance, sleepwalkers can be led back to bed and, on waking, will have no memory of their night journeys. If awakened suddenly, however, they can become frightened, alarmed, and disoriented. If shaken, they may fight back, believing, in their half-waking state, that they are being attacked.

Another memorable sleepwalking scene in opera belongs to Verdi's Lady Macbeth. Watched by her gentlewoman and doctor, she puts down the candle she carries in her sleep and begins to rub her hands as if scrubbing them clean: "Out, out, damn spot! Who would have thought the old man would have so much blood in him?" she sings, reliving in dream the murder of King Duncan. The observant Shakespeare described the condition of sleepwalking in his play in the early 17th century: Her gentlewoman reports that the sleeping Lady Macbeth "rises from her bed, throws her nightgown on herself, unlocks a closet, takes forth paper, folds it, writes upon', reads, afterwards seals it and returns to bed." The doctor remarks that her eyes are wide open, to which the gentlewoman observes, "But their sense is shut."

So it is for Bellini's Amina, who, when found in a strange man's bedroom with eyes wide open, is unaware of all that happens around her. The trusting villagers, once they get over the shock of finding her there, come to understand that this is no frightening *fantasma* but the Amina they know and love.

Characters

Amina, an orphan raised Teresa	Soprano
Elvino, a young, well-to-do farmer engaged to Amina	Tenor
Count Rodolfo, Lord of the Manor	Bass
Teresa, owner of the mill	Mezzo-soprano
Lisa, the innkeeper, in love with Elvino	Soprano

Bibliography
Sadie, Stanley, ed., *The Grove Dictionary of Opera*, Vol. 4, MacMillan Reference Ltd., London, 1998.
Sleepwalking, medical definition, www.health.com/health/centers/sleep_disorders.
Weinstock, Herbert, *Vincenzo Bellini*, Alfred A. Knopf, New York, 1971.

Beatrice & Benedict

Hector Berlioz

Love is a will o' the wisp which cometh none knows whence;
It flashes then disappears.   – Berlioz

The appeal of the music of Hector Berlioz is unique. This year, the bicentennial of his birth, the musical world is reassessing his vast repertory and bringing his three great operas back to the theatre. Berlioz loved his art with an extraordinary intensity and enthusiasm. Inspired by the writings of Goethe, Virgil, and Shakespeare, he devoted his musical career to transforming the works of these great masters into music. He is recognized today as the first true French Romantic composer, a genius rooted in the traditions of music, art, and literature. He was also one of the first superstar conductors, widely in demand all over Europe, and one of the best music critics ever. Both a dreamer and a realist, Berlioz lived his life according to his art. Tragically, he was never accepted or recognized by his own society –

his beloved Paris – and for this he suffered greatly.
Berlioz was a struggling musician of 24 when he simultaneously discovered Shakespeare and Harriet Smithson, the two great loves of his life. Smithson, a celebrated Irish Shakespearian actress, was at the height of her career when Berlioz saw her Ophelia and Juliet in Paris in 1827. He spoke no English, the language in which the Shakespearian company presented the plays, but in spite of this was profoundly affected by what he experienced. In his *Memoirs,* he recalled the first time he saw Smithson: "No actress in France ever touched, stirred, and excited the public as she did. I can only compare the effect produced by her wonderful talent, or rather her dramatic genius, on my imagination and heart, with the convulsion produced on my mind by the work of the great poet whom she interpreted." This fusing of Smithson and Shakespeare was to be an ongoing challenge for composer and actress, for Berlioz could never fully separate Smithson from the roles she played; he was in love with the characters to whom Shakespeare had given life. Reacting "In a kind of hopeless stupor," he stopped going to see the plays – they were too painful. "More experiences of that kind would have killed me," he said.

Five years after these first encounters, and after Berlioz had experienced a broken engagement with another woman, Smithson was in the audience when he conducted his *Symphonie fantastique.* He had composed the symphony about her; she was its idée fixe, its passion, its ideal. The symphony was the young composer's first full-scale work; it was also a first in the history of music for its unashamedly romantic ideas in terms of style and musical language. Berlioz described it as the translation into music of a prolonged personal experience of his love for Smithson. The composer and his beloved met a few days after the concert, declared their love, and married over the objections of both sets of parents.

Smithson's career went downhill from this point, even though Berlioz did everything he could to return her to her former glory. She was in deeply in debt, and lame from a bad fall. As time passed she grew increasingly bitter, mourned her lost fame, and became intensely jealous, accusing Berlioz of infidelity. Finally, they separated. But Berlioz's love for his Juliet and Ophelia – his muse – never died, and he supported her for the rest of her life. At her death, Liszt consoled Berlioz: "She inspired you, you sang of her; her task was done." Berlioz lived his life in a near-constant state of unrequited love; he discovered early on that music was to be his way of dealing with pain and longing, and the means of expressing his passion. He was a true Romantic.

In his youth, Berlioz composed prolifically. The great *Damnation of Faust*, a dramatic legend with full orchestra and soloists, was based on Goethe's *Faust*. Inspired by Shakespeare (and Smithson's Juliet), he composed the lovely *Romeo and Juliet* symphony, as well as the *King Lear* overture and the Fantasy on *The Tempest*. Of his three very different, operas the first, *Benvenuto Cellini*, was an *opéra semiseria* composed in the Italian style when he was 32. This work was rejected by the Opéra Comique, but played later at the Paris Opéra without success. Today it is returning to the repertory. The monumental *Les Troyens*, based on Virgil's *Aeneid*, was never played in its entirety in Berlioz's lifetime. The high point of this opera, the love duet between Dido and Aeneas, was modeled on Jessica and Lorenzo's speech from Shakespeare's *The Merchant of Venice*. The four-hour work was rejected by many theatres as being too large to mount; a badly cut version of Part Two was finally presented in Paris during Berlioz's lifetime, but with little success and to the composer's great dismay. The complete opera was not performed until 1890, 20 years after his death.

The last major composition of Berlioz' life was *Beatrice*

and Benedict, which he completed in his late fifties. Like Verdi before him, who ended his career with the amusing *Falstaff*, Berlioz chose another lighthearted Shakespearian comedy with which to end his compositional career. He wrote in his *Memoirs*: "I composed at the request of M. Bénazet, director of the casino at Baden-Baden, the comic opera in two acts *Beatrice and Benedict*. It was performed under my direction with great success at Baden-Baden in 1862. The duet, and trio between the women and Beatrice's aria all made an extraordinary impact. A few found the spoken dialogue lacking in wit. The spoken dialogue is taken almost word for word from Shakespeare's text ... " Berlioz traveled for the remaining years of his life, arranging, revising, and reviving his works. Louis, his beloved son with Harriet Smithson, died in 1867; Berlioz died in Paris two years later.

When he accepted the commission to compose *Beatrice and Benedict*, Berlioz remembered that, as a young composer, he had toyed with the idea of making an opera of Shakespeare's *Much Ado About Nothing*, and in 1852 had gone so far as to outline the plot. Now the time had come to bring the comedy to life. He had never seen the play performed on stage, but he knew the script by heart. Berlioz called Shakespeare the "great dispassionate genius, impassive as a mirror reflecting all it sees yet with the ineffable compassion he had for all things." Berlioz wrote his own libretto, staying very close to Shakespeare's original text. In the style of *opéra comique*, he composed 12 musical numbers linked by dialogue, which is how the opera is performed today.

Shakespeare's thesis in *Much Ado About Nothing* is simple: "There is a kind of merry war," he wrote, "betwixt Signor Benedict and her. They never meet but there is a skirmish of wit between them." This becomes, in Berlioz's words, "Beatrice and Benedict, who detest each other, are mutually persuaded of each other's love whereby they are inspired to true passion." That's about all there is to the plot of play and opera – much ado about nothing.

Shakespeare wrote *Much Ado* between the first and second parts of *Henry IV*, and carried over much of Falstaff's fun and wit into the comedy. Beatrice and Benedict verbally fence with each other, their words foiling and parrying, thrusting and retreating; their witty exchanges are the play's raison d'être. Benedict complains, "She speaks poniards, and every word stabs." But, it turns out, Beatrice had good cause to be upset, for Benedict had loved her before, then jilted her before going off to the wars. Small wonder Beatrice is so feisty; beneath the swift repartée, she still cares for her fickle love.

Returning from the wars, "the noble Claudio," Benedict's friend, speaks of his love for Hero, Beatrice's cousin, and then, in the next moment, asks if Hero is her father's only child. Assured that this is the case, Claudio is happy to learn he will inherit a large estate through marriage and pursues his suit with increased ardor. In Shakespeare's play, the secondary love plot of Hero and Claudio is undone by the interference of the nasty Don John, the Bastard (Shakespeare seldom minced his words), who stirs up all sorts of mischief. Berlioz left Don John's subplot out of the opera, focusing instead on the warring Beatrice and Benedict and relegating Claudio and Hero somewhat to the background.

In *Much Ado about Nothing*, the role of the watchman, Dogberry, is one of broad comedy. Shakespeare, parodying the police of his day, described Dogberry as "Man, proud man, dressed in a little brief authority." Berlioz took up Dogberry's famous exit line, "Oh, that I had been writ down an ass," and created Somarone, the singing master in the opera, a silly man whose name means "Big Donkey." Somarone is actually a combination of two of Shakespeare's characters, Dogberry and Balthasar, a rather insipid singer who, in the play, sings mournfully, "Ladies sigh no more, men were deceivers ever, to one thing constant never." Somarone fulfills the *opéra comique* requirement for a buffoon. Like Shakespeare, Berlioz had personal reasons for wanting to get back at bad musicians, bad critics, and bad singers, most of whom had maligned him at one time or another.

The story line of *Beatrice and Benedict* is straightforward. Benedict, just back from the wars, engages in a battle of wits with Beatrice from the moment he enters, while for Hero, in love with Claudio, the opera is one long preparation for their marriage. With the connivance of Hero's father, Leonato, and Don Pedro, at whose side Benedict and Claudio fought, Benedict comes to believe that Beatrice loves him; while she, overhearing a conversation between Hero and her companion, Ursula, believes that Benedict loves *her*. Somarone livens the mix with comedy until the plot resolves itself in a double marriage.

The wonder and beauty of *Beatrice and Benedict* are in its music. Berlioz himself described it as a "caprice written with the point of a needle," and there is much to listen for. The general mood is one of mild mockery, a fantasy set in a romantic dream-world. The instantly recognizable overture is a standard work heard in concert halls worldwide today. Lively and light as gossamer, it introduces two major contrasting themes from the opera, one of playfulness, the other of gentle melancholy.

The opening chorus mocks the hollow rhymes of the bad libretti so in vogue in Berlioz's time, then evolves into a dance, a *sicilienne* adapted from his very first composition, the song "Le dépit de la bergère," of 40 years earlier. In the first solo of the opera, Hero expresses her delight at Claudio's return in a lovely air, "Je vais le voir" (Soon I'll see him), which ends with a beautiful bel canto cadenza. In the duet that follows, Beatrice and Benedict taunt each other: "What, my dear Lady Disdain, are you yet living?" To which she responds, "Should my disdain ever fear to die while you are alive? You are her subsistence, her pleasure too; indeed but for you she would have no existence." There is more than a hint of bitterness in Beatrice's words. The orchestra plays with the cut-and-thrust dialogue with trills, syncopations, and all manner of dancing figures.

In a brilliant episodic trio, the independent Benedict tells Claudio and Don Pedro what he thinks of marriage, and of women in general. He assures his friends that he will never marry. "If I ever submit to the yoke of marriage, let them write a sign and set it where it points to me with these few words, 'Below you see Benedict, a married man.' " His friends laugh, unconvinced. When Somarone enters to rehearse his musicians for the wedding of Hero and Claudio, Berlioz parodies inadequate musicians as Somarone rehearses a ridiculous epithalamium, or marriage song, in which the singers propose that the happy pair die of joy. "Why survive such sweetness," they sing, in a double fugue entirely inappropriate for a wedding.

Benedict, on overhearing Don Pedro and Claudio talk about how Beatrice loves him, launches into a lively rondo, doing an about-face as he sings, none too seriously, of his newly discovered feelings, "Yes, I'll be in love. I'll love and desire, dote and admire, aspire and desire, conspire to acquire my heart's desire." Hero and Ursula end the act with one of Berlioz's most exquisite duets, "Nuit paisible et sereine" (Night, peaceful and calm). The soprano and contralto sing together, on the eve of Hero's wedding, of the beauty of the night and nature in an extraordinary mood of sweet, romantic melancholy. Gounod, overwhelmed by the beauty of the duet at its first performance, said, "Here is all that the silence of night and the serenity of nature may do to imbue the soul with tenderness and reverie."

Act II opens with preparations for the wedding feast of Hero and Claudio, and to the sounds of partying musicians offstage arguing about the finer points of wines from

Syracuse, Sicily, and Marsala. Accompanied by guitars, they trip onstage, in a generally hilarious scene, after which Beatrice sings her aria, "Dieu! Que viens-je d'entendre?"(God! What do I hear?). In complete contrast to Hero's romantic air, Beatrice thinks things through somewhat aggressively in her aria of self-discovery: "How can I believe it? Am I in love? Yes, Benedict, I adore you." The music describes her changing moods and mixed feelings. She thinks back to the sadness she felt at Benedict's departure for war, when she imagined him lying bleeding on the field of battle. Then, as trombones sing out joyously, she admits "her wild heart beats in rapture" and bids farewell to disdain, ambition, and her bitter disposition, now that love has conquered her heart. The aria builds to an impassioned cadenza that ends gently in a trio as Beatrice is joined by Hero and Ursula, who share her anticipation of the future.

Next day, caught up in the momentum of the wedding preparations of their friends, Beatrice and Benedict must face each other and own up to their feelings. This is not easy after so much merry hostility, but they somehow manage to convey to each other both indifference and hidden love in Shakespeare's marvelous lines: "A truce today, tomorrow we'll be foes again."

The final scene of the opera is the marriage of Hero and Claudio, after which the notary asks the second couple to step forward. Here Berlioz quotes Shakespeare word for word. Benedict says to Beatrice "Do you not love me?" "No more than reason," she replies. "Do you not love me?" Benedict, not to be outdone, says, "Troth no, no more than reason." Once again there is a clear breakdown in communication – until two letters by the protagonists are produced, each revealing its writer's love for the other. "Here's our own hands against our hearts!" laughs Benedict. "Come I will have you but, by this light, I take you for pity." Beatrice resists to the last: "I yield upon persuasion and partly to save your life for I was told you were very ill." From here the music catches fire and dances among the principals as their friends hang a sign: "Here you see Benedict, a married man!" The war is over, a truce is signed, and today they love. Berlioz brings the opera to a sparkling close as the finale reprises the foot-tapping music first heard in the overture.

Beatrice and Benedict is an elegant, gracefully crafted work – "bewitching," one critic described it. Though seemingly light and carefree, it has an underlying sense of romantic sadness throughout. Composition of the opera cannot have been easy for Berlioz; his second wife, Marie Recio, a singer, died during its composition, his own health was poor, and he longed for contact with his son, Louis, who was away at sea. Despite these personal difficulties, Berlioz, who lived first and foremost for his art, was able to create this bright work about the contrariness of love.

Today, Berlioz is perceived as a symbol of the ideal of the romantic artist: a man who lived passionately through his music against daunting odds. Compelled by circumstances to promote his own work for much of his life, he was bitter in his final years. Paris never accepted him, and he was disappointed and disillusioned over this neglect. In other cities, from London to St. Petersburg, he was lauded and praised, and his works were performed everywhere to critical acclaim. He was friend to the leading artists and writers of his day, among them Liszt, Chopin, Mendelssohn, Victor Hugo, and Balzac. In his work he followed the dictates of his musical heart, not the prevailing trends of musical fashion. To earn money, he became a highly respected music critic. He could not abide mediocrity, and generally said so in witty, scathing, and often amusing reviews. Many times during his life he expressed his frustration at having to write reviews when he would rather be writing music.

Financial support occasionally appeared from unlikely sources. Early in his career, Berlioz composed his *Harold en*

Italie symphony at the instigation of Paganini, who did not attend the first performances. On hearing the finished work in 1838, however, Paganini came backstage and said that he "had never been so powerfully impressed at a concert." Pulling Berlioz onstage, Paganini knelt and kissed his hands. The following day Berlioz received a letter from the famous violinist: "My dear friend, Beethoven is dead, and Berlioz alone can revive him. I have heard your divine compositions and beg you to accept, in token of my homage, 20,000 francs." For the amazed and impoverished Berlioz, this large sum of money was a miracle that freed him, for a time, from the task of writing reviews.

Berlioz composed in virtually all the classical styles: symphonies, operas, overtures, works for chorus, and songs. He enlarged the size of the symphony orchestra from the typical 60 players of the 1830s to as many as 150, a size French critics objected to as vulgar. Berlioz's works of raw genius on the grand scale influenced composers such as Wagner as to the possibilities within the orchestra of new tonal power, resources, and color. Berlioz's expanded orchestra and new techniques won him few admirers in Paris, however, who thought it presumptuous of him to try to "improve" on the classical style. Never one to pander to public opinion, Berlioz moved beyond classical harmony to explore new and innovative chord progressions in his own mercurial and often witty way. Surprisingly, he himself knew how to play only the flute and guitar. He never learned to play the piano – the whole orchestra was his instrument. His *Treatise on Instrumentation and Orchestration,* written in 1843, revolutionized performance practice; it is still used by composers and conductors today.

Berlioz traveled for much of his career, conducting his own works with new orchestras, a task that was all too often a struggle. In the *Memoirs,* Berlioz gives this account of one such encounter: "Who can imagine the tortures of rehearsals? First, the composer has to submit to the cold glances of the musicians. 'What does this Frenchman want? He should have stayed at home.' " He notices empty chairs in the orchestra. " 'The first clarinet is ill, the wife of the oboe is confined, the first violin has a sick child, the kettle drum has strained his wrist and the harp won't come 'cas he's studying his part.' " The rehearsal begins, and the notes are right about half the time, "a dreadful trial to the composer." The conductor quickens the tempo, "Then there is a nice mess, a fearful hubbub. He is forced to stop and resume the slow tempo." An argument ensues between the conductor and individual players who persist in playing wrong notes. "After three or four hours of such anti-harmonious skirmishes, everything is broken, inarticulate, out of tune, maddeningly discordant and you have to send away 60 or 80 tired and disgruntled musicians saying they don't understand this 'infernal, chaotic sort of music.' " By the third day, things begin to take a definite shape. "Then at last does the poor composer begin to breathe; the harmony becomes clear, the rhythms dart forth, the melodies smile and weep. After its first stammering attempts, the orchestra walks, talks, becomes a man! Light dawns, art appears, the thought flashes out, the work is understood and the orchestra rises, applauding and saluting the composer!"

In his final years, Berlioz realized that life would never match up to his dreams. He wrote, "I am past hopes, past illusions, past high thoughts and lofty conceptions." His passionate love for Harriet Smithson had not lasted beyond the early years, and his second marriage was not a success. At the end of his life he sought consolation in another dream with Estelle, a young girl with whom he had first fallen in love at the age of 12, but this too was doomed to disappointment: When he met her again, she was widowed and old, and more than a little confused at the passionate old friend from her childhood who appeared on her doorstep.

Berlioz found consolation at last, not in his muses but in Shakespeare, and found it in his heart and creative genius to write lightly of much ado about nothing and the vicissitudes of love. Composing the lively *Beatrice and Benedict*, Berlioz looks back to the passion and fire of his youthful relationship with Harriet Smithson, his Juliet and Ophelia, who later became the argumentative Beatrice. In Hero he may have looked back wistfully to what might have been had he found a blissful, uncomplicated love. But that was not to be; in the end, Berlioz cast off sad thoughts to ask, philosophically, "Which of two powers can elevate man to the sublime heights? It is a great problem yet, it seems to me, that while love can give no idea of music, music can give an idea of love, why separate them? They are two wings of the soul."

Characters

Leonato, Governor of Messina	Speaking role
Hero, his daughter	Soprano
Beatrice, her cousin	Mezzo-soprano or soprano
Don Pedro, Prince of Aragon	Bass
Benedict	Tenor
Claudio	Baritone
Somarone, singing master	Bass
Ursula, Hero's companion	Mezzo-soprano

Bibliography

Barzun, Jacques, *Berlioz and the Romantic Century*, Vol. 2, Little, Brown and Co., Boston, 1950

Berlioz, Hector, *Memoirs of Hector Berlioz*, translated by D. Newman, Dover Publications, Inc., New York, 1966

Macdonald, Hugh, *Berlioz*, Master Musicians series, Stanley Sadie, ed., Oxford University Press, 2000

Sadie, Stanley, ed., *Grove Dictionary of Opera*, Vol. 1, Macmillan Reference Ltd., London, 1998